PROBLEM-SOLVING IN GROUPS

PROBLEM-SOLVING IN GROUPS
Third edition

Mike Robson

GOWER

Published by
Gower Publishing Limited
Gower House
Croft Road
Aldershot
Hampshire GU11 3HR
England

Gower
131 Main Street
Burlington VT 05401–5600 USA

British Library Cataloguing in Publication Data
Robson, Mike, 1944–
    Problem-solving in groups. – 3rd ed.
    1. Problem-solving 2. Teams in the workplace 3. Group decision
    making 4. Management
    I. Title
    658.4'036

Library of Congress Control Number: 2002100272

ISBN 0 566 08467 8

Typeset in 10 on 12 Garamond Light by Bournemouth Colour Press, Parkstone and printed in Great Britain by MPG Books Limited, Bodmin.

CONTENTS

PREFACE

The use of properly trained and equipped problem-solving groups as a mechanism for organizational improvement and individual involvement and development has grown massively over the past 20 years or so.

This is the third edition of *Problem-solving in Groups*. It has sold many thousands of copies, in both its standard form and also customized for use in a wide range of individual companies. It has been translated into most European languages as well as others as diverse as Russian, Mandarin and Indonesian.

The book presents a logical problem-solving process and contains many tools and techniques to assist groups to identify, analyze and solve problems successfully. Some of these techniques are commonly used, others are less well known and some are original. (Chapter 5, pages 35–37, provides more detail of what tools and techniques appear in which chapters.)

This edition is updated and is presented in a new format. There are also two significant additions. The first deals with the rapidly emerging phenomenon of working in 'virtual' teams (Chapter 4) where some of the issues involved in group working are changed or at least heightened, though the underlying structure of problem-solving can remain. The second is a chapter on facilitating problem-solving groups. This is a role which is increasingly recognized as being key to the success of strategies aimed at involvement and improvement of organizational performance.

Problem-solving in Groups is meant to be read but, more importantly, used by anyone engaged in this activity whether they be facilitators, leaders or members of problem-solving groups, or indeed, anyone who has an interest in the problem-solving process. It has been written in a style that is simple to understand and its contents are adaptable for use as training material where necessary.

The intention of the book is to provide organizations and their people with a structure that will help them to achieve substantial results as they work on the process of continuous improvement. In addition I hope that it will motivate people to get involved, through providing a systematic step-by-step process, and add to the job satisfaction of everyone who chooses to use their energies in this way for the benefit of their organization and their own development.

As ever, thank you Bee.

Mike Robson

PART I
INTRODUCTION

❖

1

AN INTRODUCTION TO GROUP PROBLEM-SOLVING

How could we have been so stupid? (John F. Kennedy on reviewing his cabinet's decision-making process after the Bay of Pigs fiasco)

There are many problems that can only be solved by effective group working. However, it is important to recognize that there are just as many that are far better tackled by an individual. This book does not in any way seek to persuade the reader that groups are the best way of doing everything. There are all too many examples of misplaced group working leading to failure, frustration and wasted time, effort and money. The ability to recognize situations where a group approach will prove beneficial is important, and then it is vital to ensure that those working in the group are equipped to work effectively together. This book is about these issues.

INDIVIDUAL OR GROUP?

At the outset it will be useful to establish clearly the occasions when both individual and group working will be the best option. Certainly there is no point in setting up a group if the problem or issue to be resolved has one answer that can be diagnosed more quickly and effectively by one person, and where there is no requirement for others to understand or be committed to the solution. Equally, there is no point if the decision has been made already and the group is being manipulated into rubber-stamping the decision; groups have a habit of seeing through such ploys and reacting adversely to them. This all sounds very simple and obvious but many groups have been established that fall into exactly these traps.

WHEN TO USE A GROUP

Group problem-solving is the best way of tackling issues in three main circumstances.

First, there are many problems that concern more than one person. In such situations, each of those involved is likely to have a legitimate view, and it is always wise to take these different perceptions into account in arriving at the solution. Secondly, there are problems where there is no straightforward single answer, and the right approach needs to be an amalgam of the views of different people. Thirdly, there are situations where it is important that those involved are committed to the solution, and sometimes this is more relevant than the solution itself. In practice, there are an increasing number of situations where one or other of these circumstances are the key, which is why group problem-solving has become so much more important as a strategy for improvement in the past few years. There are a number of very real advantages that group problem-solving offers when it is used in the right situations and with properly equipped people.

THE ADVANTAGES OF GROUP PROBLEM-SOLVING

'Many hands make light work', and there is no doubt that having a number of minds attuned to a problem will improve both the discussion and the decision as long as they use a rigorous problem-solving process, are committed and work effectively together. Given this there is no reason why everyone in the organization should not be involved in such activities. All of these elements are of real importance and need to be understood.

ANALYTICAL AND CREATIVE THINKING

We tend to think analytically rather than creatively, and individually rather than collectively. This approach is often both appropriate and successful when the problem being considered is amenable to it. There are many other occasions, however, when this approach seems to achieve little. Many problems in organizations are not new; they are perennial issues that have been tackled before, but always seem to re-emerge. Often the best available analytical minds have been put to work on such problems, but to no avail. Why is this?

The reality is that some issues cannot be solved by the application of pure logic; they need a different, more creative approach. This does not imply that the disciplines of the analytical approach need be lost, however, since what is required is a process that uses the best of both problem-solving styles. The process described in this book is an ideal combination of the rigours of the analytical method in that it is based on collecting facts rather than opinions, and the benefits of the creative approach which generates many different ideas, forces the exploration of issues from all angles and looks at unusual possibilities as well as obvious ones.

COMMITMENT

Commitment is probably an overused word but we all know how important it is, and a further general advantage of the group problem-solving approach is that there will be a significant higher level of commitment to the final solution amongst those that have taken part in generating it. We all know from our own experience that we are most enthusiastic about our own ideas, or those that we have at least had a say in. Many problems and opportunities for improvement involve more than one person, section or department, and it is likely that these different parties will have different views; indeed, this is often the problem! In such circumstances there is often no obvious single right answer and the group approach is the only one that stands a chance of success since it is structured to take into account the views of everyone.

Many seemingly impossible problems have been resolved by involving the interested parties in developing the solution using an orderly problem-solving process. This approach has worked not just because of the technicalities of the solution but because those involved have been committed to the solution that they themselves devised. Arguably, there are today many situations where this kind of commitment is the single most important factor in achieving success. Committed people will often make things work that otherwise would fail.

THE IMPORTANCE OF UNDERSTANDING GROUP WORKING

If they are to be successful members of problem-solving groups need to be skilled in working together. It is remarkable that so little attention is paid to this subject. It is, more often than not, assumed that we know how to work together effectively as if such skills were innate. The reality is very different. We all know of groups of the most talented people that have not delivered to their capability; indeed, sometimes such groups have gone disastrously wrong. A classic example of this occurred when John F. Kennedy was the president of the USA. He surrounded himself with a Cabinet that was commonly recognized as the most intellectually capable in history and yet they stumbled into a number of crises, the most serious of which were the Cuban missile crisis and the Bay of Pigs fiasco, which could easily have caused a nuclear war. After the crisis had been averted, at the eleventh hour, and when President Kennedy reflected on the way he and his cabinet had handled the events he said, 'How could we have been so stupid?'

Most of us are not in situations which threaten the stability of the world, but we are involved with the survival and success of our organizations. We also know that there are occasions when we, and others in our organizations, end up in situations that we really do not want to be in, so it is important that we understand the reasons why this happens.

Basically, such situations occur because groups very often have an insufficient understanding of the 'dynamics' that are affecting their working together. We tend to be very task oriented, to get on with the job in hand, to work at it and to see it through. In fact, most people are 'task-mesmerized'; they cannot see anything else other than the issues that relate directly to the problem itself. This ability to focus single-mindedly has generally been seen as a strength and yet it is often unsuccessful. The reality is that most difficulties and impediments that face problem-solving groups are not related to the task at all, but to the way that the group is working. The subject of group process or group dynamics is vast and it would be impractical to expect everyone to become an expert. It is essential, however, that anyone who becomes involved in group working also becomes acquainted with at least the basics of the subject if they are to avoid the many traps that will prevent the group from successfully completing its work. These basics are included as a key part of the process described in this book.

EVERYONE CAN BE INVOLVED

A further benefit of group problem-solving using the process recommended in this book is that people from every level of the organization can play their part.

Every director, manager or executive should have these skills. If they do not, why should their employees? There is no requirement for academic qualifications or special organizational experience. Equipping employees to be able to contribute to the improvement process by playing their part in such groups helps to utilize the real experience, knowledge and talent that exists in the organization. Ultimately, there is nothing to prevent everyone being trained and then given the opportunity to join in problem-solving and other improvement activities. Indeed, this should be the aim. Do not fall into the trap of thinking that only certain people will be worth training, that some will not want to join in, or that others will not be able to handle it. The process and the techniques in this book have been used successfully by people from a wide variety of backgrounds and at all levels of thousands of organizations worldwide.

SUMMARY

In this chapter we have looked at a number of issues to do with when to use groups to solve problems, the advantages when you do so in the right circumstances and the major benefit that everyone in the organization can be involved. This is an increasingly important aspect of organizations in the twenty-first century.

2

GROUP PROBLEM-SOLVING IN THE TWENTY-FIRST CENTURY

Change is now the only constant. (Alvin Toffler)

In organizations all over the world there have been a number of developments in the past few years that have brought the subject of group problem-solving to the forefront as an important part of organizational strategy. They are:

○ continuous improvement
○ participation
○ managing business processes.

CONTINUOUS IMPROVEMENT

In a world that is changing at breakneck speed it is obvious that standing still is, in fact, going backwards. As Alvin Toffler said in his book, *Future Shock*, 'change is now the only constant'. Furthermore change is happening at an increasingly exponential rate. Because of this it is clear that every organization that wishes to survive, let alone succeed, must have continuous improvement as a fundamental part of its strategy.

Put bluntly, if you do not improve you do not survive.

As products and services become more sophisticated and complex, and as customer expectations rise and competition increases, traditional ways of doing things are increasingly not good enough. What is needed are

9

mechanisms for improvement and tools to refocus people away from the 'test and fix', 'you can't win 'em all', firefighting approach of the past to a way of doing things that is truly based on prevention, thus avoiding the need to spend time on remedial work. Part of this philosophy includes recognizing that if and when things do go wrong they need to be put right permanently, not simply patched over.

Problem-solving groups have a vital role in the continuous improvement process, first by solving the problems of the past properly and permanently, and second in creating solutions that are robust and that are adaptable to the certainty of even more change in the future.

PARTICIPATION

The recognition that employees at all levels of the organization have more to contribute than just the strength of their arms and legs is not new, but historically even employers who believed this have not always found it easy to turn the belief into a practical reality. There are four keys to success in achieving widespread and effective participation. One of the most beneficial forms of employee participation is involvement in problem-solving groups since they not only work on important issues that are affecting the performance of the organization, but also improve the working relationships between people which, of course, also affect the performance of the organization.

CULTURE

The first key is for the organization to develop a culture which expects people from all levels to be actively involved in the process of improvement, not just occasionally but every day and in every way. This means that it is not just up to management, or a group of selected employees, to find ways of making things better, it is a natural part of everyone's job, something in which all employees can help to ensure the ongoing survival and success of their organization.

VOLUNTARY

The second key is that, even within a culture that expects participation, involvement in particular activities should, wherever possible, be on a voluntary basis. We all know that we tend to be most enthusiastic when we want to engage in the particular endeavour, rather than being pressed into it. When we want to do something we are much more likely to make sure we work at it and gain success.

TRAINING

Third, it is essential that people are trained in the tools and the skills that are needed to solve problems successfully and to realize sustainable improvements. It is a recipe for disaster if people are encouraged to contribute but then find that their efforts are rejected, or even ignored, because they amount to little more than poorly thought through opinions.

RECOGNITION

Fourth, it needs to be recognized that it is neither natural nor easy to develop a culture of ongoing participation in improvement, especially when it applies to our own work area. We can all see clearly why and how others can improve but because we are working hard and 'doing our best' it is much harder for us to see our own need. Therefore, there is a requirement for an ongoing way of publicizing results and giving recognition to those who have been involved. The first of these is similar in principle to a marketing campaign, but one that focuses inward to the employees in the organization rather than outward to the end customer. As far as recognition is concerned there are many ways of structuring such a scheme as long as the recognition is both public and tangible. The private 'pat on the back' is fine and to be encouraged, but the feeling wears off very quickly and so needs to be supported with other mechanisms. In designing such schemes it should be noted that recognition is different from reward (usually money), and for most people is actually valued more highly.

MANAGING BUSINESS PROCESSES

The final development in understanding the keys to survival and success has been the increasing realization that a key to progress today lies in understanding and improving the business processes used by organizations, rather than the conventional approach of focusing on working within functional hierarchies. Business processes are the flows of work, passing from internal supplier to internal customer, through the organization.

The conventional approach sees the organization as a series of 'functional drainpipes', for example, marketing, sales, finance, information technology (IT), with a huge amount of energy being used in the management of each of these. It is only relatively recently that it was realized that 'real work' does not go up and down these hierarchies, rather it flows across them in a series of business processes that involve more than one function. Historically these had been left entirely unmanaged in any overall sense, on the assumption that if the functions were managed all would be well.

As we now know, this is not the case. Many of the problems faced by organizations today are as a direct result of unproductive cross-functional rivalry, or are issues that fall somewhere in the grey area between the responsibilities of different departments, 'the bits between the boxes' of the organization chart.

A range of techniques has been developed to help people address these issues and these techniques all depend on effective group working since, in situations such as these, it is not only the solution that matters but also the understanding and commitment of those who are involved with, and actually operate, the process in question.

In one case the catering department in a large hospital was criticized by patients and staff alike for the fact that the food they were serving was invariably cold and therefore spoiled when it arrived at the bedside. A group was set up to look at the problem and after employing the problem-solving process realized that the catering department thought that its responsibility was to deliver the food (hot) to the door of the ward where they were to leave it for the nursing staff to collect and deliver to the patient. The nursing staff believed that the caterers were either lazy or embarrassed about the quality of the food and that this was why they left it at the door of the ward. The nurses were also often busy and so the food got left until someone found it and wheeled it in, at which point it was ruined. Once this was realized the problem was easy to solve – it is a simple illustration of a failure to manage a cross-functional business process.

SUMMARY

There is no doubt that process management is vital since so many problems are caused by cross-functional difficulties. It is also the case that encouraging people to engage in the process of continuous improvement is a major key to success in the modern world.

3

PROBLEM-SOLVING GROUPS

A problem shared is a problem halved.

There are four different kinds of conventional problem-solving groups and it is important that we distinguish them at the outset. The past few years have also seen the emergence of an important fifth type, the 'virtual' group which, by its nature, is different and is dealt with in a separate chapter.

TASK FORCES AND DEPARTMENT GROUPS

The first two types of group are task forces and department groups. They are similar in every respect except that a task force is a cross-functional group usually set up by a senior manager, or the senior management team, whereas a department group is a group established by the manager in a department or section to solve a local problem, and generally contains members of the department, though it is possible to include others with relevant knowledge and skills where appropriate.

SPECIFIC ISSUES

The first feature of a task force or department group is that it is a group formed to look at a specific issue which a manager believes is important and warrants investigation by a group.

OWNERSHIP

The second feature of this type of group concerns ownership. With these groups, the real ownership rests with the person that initiated the activity. This is an important feature to bear in mind with any group activity, since it is likely to affect the underlying commitment that people have towards the subject in hand. The main purpose here is to have an important issue investigated in a thorough manner by a group of suitably qualified employees.

MEMBERSHIP

The selection of members of the group is the third feature to note, and the key here is to understand that people are told that they will be a part of activity. Of course, the wise manager will ensure that the people chosen for membership are encouraged and helped to be interested in the project, but inevitably the people to do the job will be chosen according to their potential contribution as far as this particular problem or issue is concerned.

FORMULATION

The fourth feature of these groups is that the precise formulation will vary according to the particular issue being investigated, but in terms of size it should never exceed the traditionally accepted limits of a small group, which is to say ten people, but more normally seven. If more than ten people are involved in a problem-solving activity, the dynamics of the group become very complex, and invariably reduce the effectiveness of the work accomplished.

Task forces and department groups can be used in a wide range of situations. It is likely in organizations of any size that there will always be such groups operating as new issues, problems and opportunities need to be addressed. As a device they are similar to project groups which are used already by many organizations, but they have a distinct advantage over the majority of such activities in that members of the group will be trained in, and will use, a problem-solving structure. An essential requirement for all these group activities is that members are trained in how to identify, analyze and solve problems, how to work together effectively in groups, how to present their findings and how to monitor and evaluate results.

IMPROVEMENT TEAMS

Improvement teams are the third type of group. Perhaps the most important feature of such teams lies in the fact that the group consists entirely of volunteers who work in the same department or work group. This, of course, gives the ownership of the group to the members, and this is further reinforced by the members of the group having the responsibility for selecting which problems they wish to tackle from within their department. Other important features of this approach are that the supervisor or first-level manager is the leader of the group, especially at the start, and that the activity involves a natural working group, not a selection of people from different departments and functions. Finally, improvement teams are not designed to be ad hoc problem-solving groups that disband having tackled one issue – they are there to put their own house in order and to maintain it; these are ongoing activities.

ISSUE TEAMS

The fourth type of group is the issue team. People in organizations are not solely concerned with issues and problems that only affect them. There are many other opportunities for improvement that are of interest, but they require other people to be involved as well if any progress is to be made. In short, there is a need for a mechanism that allows employees, including management, to work on issues of interest and concern to them, in groups which they own. Improvement teams fulfil this requirement within the natural work group, whilst issue teams deal with it where the need goes across departmental or functional boundaries.

VOLUNTARY MEMBERSHIP

The first important aspect of issue teams is that, like improvement teams, membership is voluntary, which means that there is a far greater likelihood of the people who join in being committed to the group, the problem and the process. A practical expression of the voluntary nature is in the vesting of ownership with the group. Within the broad guidelines set down, group members are free to explore the subject of their concern.

SPECIFIC ISSUES

The second notable feature is that issue teams are based on specific issues. These can be problems or opportunities; it does not matter. The important point to note is that the group forms to look at one issue. Once the issue has been dealt with, the group disbands. With a task force, the timescale involved in exploring the issue selected by management is unlikely to be more than a few months in most circumstances, and there will be improvement teams for which this is also the case. There are likely to be other subjects, however, which necessitate the group continuing its activity for a much longer period of time, and indeed there may be some which need to be ongoing. To a large extent the issue itself will determine this since, with a voluntary group, membership will quickly fall away once the job has been done and there is therefore no remaining interest in the work.

It should be stated, however, that the members of issue teams, because it is their group, can continue to meet for as long as they think fit, and as long as they perceive there is value in pursuing the topic further. So, unlike improvement teams, the group does not select another problem to work on once the initial problem has been solved. Members of the group may, of course, opt to be members of another issue team that forms to work on a different challenge, but the original group disbands once its job has been done.

COMPOSITION

The third aspect of issue teams concerns their composition. As far as members are concerned, the only limit should be that of a small group – up to ten people. The group should be allowed to meet for a maximum of one hour per week, and the understanding should be that members should spend less time if they believe it to be appropriate. An important aspect of these groups is that everyone in the organization ultimately should be given the chance to belong to one, since they represent a very useful way of encouraging the involvement of all staff and of developing commitment to solving a wide range of organizational problems. The membership of these groups does not usually come just from one work area; they are, more often than not, cross-functional. Furthermore, representation from different levels in the organization, including management, should be encouraged wherever possible and appropriate. This not only helps to ensure a rounded analysis and proposal for improvement, but also helps to reinforce communication up and down the organization as well as across the functional boundaries. An important characteristic of the success of issue teams is that they are task-oriented groups that use a systematic problem-solving structure to ensure a professional treatment of their subjects; they do not merely talk around matters.

DIFFERENCES BETWEEN THE GROUPS

The main differences between these groups relate therefore to who has the real ownership and to whether or not the group is departmental or cross-functional. Only improvement teams are designed to be ongoing; the others will disband after solving the problem at hand.

All four groups have a role to play in the process of improving the performance of the organization, and they all use the same basic problem-solving process that is covered in this book. The process provides an appropriate blend of creative and analytical tools that will enable the group to think both imaginatively and rigorously.

Each type of group should consist of between four and ten people, with the ideal being seven. Group meetings should be held regularly once a week and last an hour. We all know that time is a scarce resource and it is an important part of the deployment of such groups that they are disciplined enough to achieve what they need to in the time available. The meetings, wherever possible, are held during the normal working day. Occasionally there will be situations which mean that the group can only meet outside normal hours, but this is to be avoided if possible. Experience shows that the groups themselves are in the best position to decide when they meet, and to ensure that any disruption is kept to a minimum.

Occasionally, management will decide that an issue needs to be tackled quickly and will increase the frequency of the meetings or their length. It is worth noting, however, that the one hour a week works well and tends not to disrupt normal work patterns.

RESPONSIBILITIES OF PROBLEM-SOLVING GROUPS

A further important point is that all of these types of group are responsible for the full problem-solving process. To be successful they all have to define the problem precisely, to analyze the issue, collect and interpret relevant data, generate possible solutions, calculate the costs and benefits, select a solution and sell it to management. If management then gives approval, it is also usually the job of the group to implement its solution, monitor results and make sure the problem does not recur. Because these groups are given the chance to tackle problems from beginning to end, the group members obtain greater satisfaction, and more problems get fixed and stay fixed.

SUMMARY

An important aspect of successful group problem-solving is knowing that there are different types of groups that are configured for particular circumstances. Many groups have become confused and even despondent because they have been given inaccurate expectations of their immediate and ongoing role.

4

PROBLEM-SOLVING IN 'VIRTUAL TEAMS'

Hands across the sea.

Over the past few years, since the Internet has begun to affect more of us in both our private and working lives, a new type of group has begun to be used, especially by organizations that have a wide geographical spread or those who work extensively with partners who are based in different areas or countries. They are generally called 'virtual' teams to signify the fact that they are working as a group or team, yet they rarely, if ever, meet face to face. Though the issues that affect such teams are not nearly as well researched as for conventional teams, some very useful work has been done which can be of great help in making such activities successful. It goes without saying that such teams are different and, though many of the issues that affect them are the same as for normal groups, there is often a need to adapt the way we handle them. This applies primarily to managing the dynamics of such teams but some of the problem-solving techniques are also affected in these circumstances, for example a brainstorming session held by a 'virtual' team is unlikely to be as fast and furious as one where everyone is in the same room. Having said that, in other respects the technique should be handled in just the same way as described in the chapter on the subject.

THE NEED FOR TRAINING

What is certain is that unless such teams are taught how to work well together in this configuration, and are trained in the basic techniques of problem-solving, they will not succeed. This is made all the more important when we realize that the issues being dealt with in this way are likely to be critical ones, and the level of personnel being utilized quite senior. Such problem-solving teams will generally be task forces, involving people from different parts of the organization, who are given the task of solving an important problem that is affecting, or could affect, the performance of the organization. Other 'virtual' teams will be drawn together for a variety of purposes, such as working on global bids or proposals. These are not problem-solving groups as defined in this book, but the issues dealt with here concerning the management of the dynamics of the team are just as critical to any 'virtual' team whatever its purpose.

THE MAIN ISSUES IN VIRTUAL TEAMS

Virtual teams face many of the same difficulties as do other more conventional groups but they express themselves in different ways. There are also other issues which are particular to such groups. Experience to date indicates that the main points to focus on are as follows:

- trust
- goals
- communication
- roles
- motivation and urgency
- process review
- organization culture.

These are dealt with in the rest of this chapter.

TRUST – THE KEY ISSUE

Many of us will have been involved at the formation of a new group which was set up to deal with a sensitive issue. During the first one or two meetings we will have thought to ourselves, 'what we are dealing with here is not only sensitive, it is tricky and potentially dangerous from a personal point of view. I have to be careful what I say and do until I can be sure that I can trust the others in the group. And I'm not at all sure about the one that wears yellow ties!'

In this situation we can see the others in the group, we can evaluate their body language and we can take whatever precautions we want to on the basis of the evidence we believe we have seen. Trust is a major issue in all groups, especially at the outset. If it is not handled well and the group does not develop mutual trust, it will most certainly fail since members will not be prepared to 'risk' themselves in the service of the best outcome for the group.

Given that this is the case in traditional groups it is clear that the issue of trust is even more of an issue in virtual teams. We cannot see the other members. We may not know them or even have met them, and we are being asked to work together on a problem which could affect our reputation and our career in the organization. It is therefore essential that the issue of trust is dealt with both carefully and successfully.

HANDLING THE TRUST ISSUE

There is no doubt that the best way to develop trust in a virtual team is to have a face-to-face meeting of the members. This is of course paradoxical in that virtual teams are ones where members work remotely from each other, but there is no available human or other technology that is nearly as good. Not only can important things to do with the nature and the running of the group be worked out, but the often unrecognized place of social interaction can be accommodated. Having a meal together and chatting at the bar is good fun but it is much more than that in terms of setting levels of trust, cooperation and mutual support within the group. Video conferencing has its place, for example, but there is nothing to match being able to 'eyeball' other members of the group – and them you of course!

Cost of course is a major issue here, but if the problem or issue being dealt with is of sufficient importance for such a group to have been set up in the first place an initial investment of a one-, or preferably two-day initial, face-to-face meeting will be well worthwhile. There is an increasingly commonly held view that it is actually essential since so many of the difficulties that beset virtual teams can be avoided, solved or ameliorated if such a meeting is agreed and then well thought through, rigorously conducted and expertly facilitated. A suggested agenda for such a meeting is included at the end of this chapter.

If a face-to-face meeting is simply not possible, and there should not be many occasions when this is the case, the issue of trust will have to be handled 'virtually'. In this case it is absolutely essential that the team leader confronts the issue at the outset. In this circumstance it will probably not be wise to start with an announcement that 'we have a problem with trust within the group'. We make our judgements about whether or not we trust someone on the basis of our beliefs about what we see and hear so the leader in this situation should be concerned about the sharing of useful, relevant and revealing information between team members. The nature of the information that is solicited to be shared amongst all will, of course, be influenced by the culture of the organization, the type and level of the people involved and the nature of the issue which is to be addressed. The leader in deciding what questions to ask should remember that this first objective is to try to develop the first stages of a mutually trusting environment within which the group can operate successfully. For example:

○   name
○   age
○   domestic situation
○   role in the organization
○   perception of the most important aspect of the current role
○   ambitions within the organization
○   outside interests
○   key values
○   what do I like most in people/organizations?
○   what do I dislike most in people/organizations?

The list is potentially endless and must be managed to be appropriate and also not too time-consuming or daunting, but it must make sense in the context of sharing information which will help to create an atmosphere of trust.

ACTION IMPROVES TRUST

Research into 'virtual' teams indicates clearly that there are a number of things that the leader and members can do which will help the creation of a more trusting environment. These largely relate to people using their individual initiative. Volunteer, do not just ask for volunteers, suggest, do not just ask for suggestions, be actively positive, not complaining, respond calmly in the face of difficulties. Finally, remember that action in itself tends to improve trust.

GOALS – WHAT ARE WE HERE TO DO?

The next major issue concerns goals. Almost every group has at least a potential problem in gaining a mutual and agreed understanding of what it is there to achieve. Most have an actual problem because, remarkably, there is usually very little common agreement over the objectives of the group. Briefs are given in vague and general terms, individual members take their own interpretations of these briefs and often, because of the assumption that everyone must be of the same mind, nothing is clarified and the result is disaster! There is certainly a very clear need for a process of stating, clarifying and agreeing what the group is trying to achieve.

HOW TO CLARIFY GOALS

In a 'virtual' team this will have to be initiated and guided by the leader and will be an iterative process which may take a number of iterations. The key is to ask each individual member to state from the initial brief what they perceive to be the key aspects of it and what, fundamentally, the group is there to achieve. All the answers should be posted for everyone to see and then another round initiated, allowing people to gain from the perceptions of other group members in refining their own view. This may have to be done a number of times and the leader may need to reinforce that this is not time-wasting; that unless they are clear about their mutual goal, they will never be successful. It should be said, though, that this part of the process should be dealt with at speed so that members do not get frustrated with what might appear to be non-productive activity.

The leader in this process has a vital role in summarizing views, bringing them together and proposing possible goal statements that are clear, succinct, accurate and detailed enough to be useful. A major danger lies in taking many inputs and generalizing them to the point that they are merely platitudes, for example, 'communication', 'attitudes' and 'working conditions'. The leader should not stop this part of the problem-solving process until there is complete agreement, stated in writing (which can include email) from all group members, of the goal of the group. It is much better, if it comes to it, to lose a member of the group at this stage than to prejudice the effectiveness of later work. Having said this, always remember the value of unconventional thinkers – they often have much to give, however difficult they are to manage.

COMMUNICATION

The issue termed as 'communication' is the most often cited as being the main problem in groups, and organizations. In 'virtual' teams, because we cannot see each other, the issue is made more pronounced and so special efforts are needed to handle it. There are practical things that can be done. These can be divided into actions that are useful at the outset of a 'virtual' team and those which are useful in its middle and later stages.

INITIAL COMMUNICATION THAT CAN INCREASE TRUST

There is no denying that the leader of any 'virtual' team faces a daunting task. At the outset it is important, and there is an opportunity, to establish a basic 'ethos' with which we want to surround the operation. Initial communications with members should, more than anything, be enthusiastic about the nature and purpose of the group. Leaders should also be aware of the importance of social interaction in all teams and should make it easily possible for people to share their interests even in this difficult, 'virtual', format. From the leader's point of view it is as if we are trying to have a conversation at the bar whilst being in ten different countries – hard, but not impossible by any means. Encourage members to share their interests, goals, family details, out-of-work hobbies and so on from the outset. This will help to build a 'social' infrastructure within which the group will operate much more effectively.

Do not underestimate the importance of these steps.

ONGOING COMMUNICATION REQUIREMENTS

In the 'normal' course of events we are able readily to observe and take a view about whether people in the group are interested, motivated and keen to play their part. In 'virtual' teams it is undoubtedly more difficult and so there are some requirements that need to be made part of the fabric of such operations, specifically that communication should be predictable, substantive and timely.

Predictable communication

The first fundamental need is for communication that is predictable. This need can be accommodated if the communication is at first regular, then informative and, finally, that it contains no major surprises.

As far as regular communication is concerned most of us know the feelings of frustration as we wait for an overdue email. Has the other party received ours, forgotten or simply lost interest? The implication of this is that we must ensure a regular flow of information within the 'virtual' team.

Second we need to ensure that the communications within the team are informative. I look forward to emails from my friends, but when they come and say, 'Hi how are you, what news do you have for me?' I tend to think that they are not adding much to my life!

Third, as far as possible, there should be no major surprises. There are 'bolts from the blue' in the best run organizations, but as far as possible communication about relevant issues within the team should be ongoing so that no big issues 'come out of the woodwork' to surprise and disturb members.

Substantive communication

It is also vital that the communication within a 'virtual' team is substantive. I was in such a team once and, having received a fairly detailed report and proposal from a member half-way through the project, I sent an email back which said 'Received your communication'. The other party expressed dissatisfaction with this in no uncertain terms – I was, 'uninterested, unconcerned, uncommitted'.

I had actually read it, but had not said so. I had taken a view about it, but had not shared it. Actually I had things that I wanted to add and amend but had not done so. These were in my mind, but how was my colleague to know?

The clear lesson here is that when working in a 'virtual' team make sure that your replies make it clear that previous correspondence has been studied and also that you add useful inputs rather than simply saying that you have received and noted the contents. If you have nothing to add, pick out something that you particularly agree with or that you think is especially worthwhile and feed this back; it will be worth it in terms of the smooth and effective running of the group.

Timely communication

One of the potentially most frustrating things about working in a 'virtual' team is waiting for a response from another member when we do not even know whether our communication has been received, let alone read, understood or agreed with. We tend to make assumptions in our mind relating to lack of interest and motivation, even trust, if replies are not forthcoming quickly enough for our liking. It is therefore very important when setting up a 'virtual' team that agreements are made at the outset concerning the speed of response of individuals to inputs from others. It should also be a normal part of the working routine that a time schedule is included for tasks to be achieved, that is, who will do what, by when, and that the ethic of the group is always to meet these deadlines. There is ample evidence that trust, motivation and interest will rapidly decay if this is not in place.

ROLES

Belbin's work on team roles, with which many will be familiar, shows us that we all have preferred roles that we bring to any group that we belong to. In summary these roles are as follows:

○   chairperson – clarifies goals and priorities, motivates colleagues
○   shaper – challenges, pressurizes, finds ways round obstacles

O   company worker – turns ideas and plans into practical forms of action

O   plant – creates original ideas, solves difficult problems

O   resource investigator – explores new possibilities, develops contacts, negotiates

O   monitor evaluator – sees all options, judges likely outcomes accurately

O   team worker – listens, builds, averts friction, handles difficult people

O   completer/finisher – searches for errors, omissions and oversights, concentrates on and keeps others to schedules and targets.

A fuller explanation of team roles is given in Chapter 17, 'Facilitating problem-solving groups'.

A successful group needs all of these roles and no one person provides them all. Most of us contribute one primary role and perhaps one or two secondary roles. For example, someone may be good at creating ideas, developing contacts and negotiating, but hopeless at getting things done on time. It is easy to see the potential value of the positive contribution such a person could make and equally clear is the damage that could be done. It is worthwhile, therefore, at the start to make this a 'live' issue. If the group is able to meet at the start of its work there are simple questionnaires available that will help members to share their preferred team roles as a prelude to discussing their implications for the group in question. (A good, professional source of this material can be obtained from the www.dulewicz.com website, which can also assist with analysis.) If the group cannot meet, it will be worthwhile for the leader at the very least to post the roles and definitions and to ask members to assess and share their own perception of their primary and secondary roles.

MOTIVATION AND URGENCY IN 'VIRTUAL' TEAMS

In the majority of cases 'virtual' teams will be established to fulfil a specific and important function which, once addressed, will lead to the disbanding of the group. The implication of this is that usually membership of such a body will be a part-time occupation to be worked on whilst still performing in the main job. It is important to bear this in mind since it may well have implications for the sense of urgency that people bring to the task and also for their overall level of motivation in putting energy into it. To achieve the necessary levels of both to give the project a chance of success the initial set-up will be vital.

First, the importance of the project will have to be made clear and stressed, preferably by a senior person in the organization. Part of this should be to make clear why the issue is important and what benefits a successful conclusion will bring. Second, the membership of the group should be explained in the sense that the chosen members are seen as being those that can deliver rather than those who have time on their hands to spend on the activity. Third, it will be wise for the senior sponsor to explain how closely in touch with progress he or she will be during the life of the group.

If this is done well when the 'virtual' team begins its work there is likely to be a high level of initial enthusiasm, but this can dissipate very quickly unless rapid progress is made. Individual members and especially the leader can assist in this. We have already mentioned how advisable it is to hold an initial face-to-face meeting as so much can be achieved in a relatively short space of time if such an event is planned and facilitated well. If it is not possible, the same issues will have to be dealt with but in a more difficult, 'virtual' format.

SHIFT FROM PROCEDURAL TO TASK ISSUES

At the start of any group it is necessary to establish the rules and procedures that will be used. This is vital but, of course, it is not the reason the group was formed. The key here, then, is to get the necessary infrastructure agreed and in place quickly, efficiently and properly, to clear the way for the group to focus on the task at hand. If this stage goes on too long members will become frustrated and lose interest. Even in conventional groups discussions about such issues can quickly become convoluted, and this is even more the case in 'virtual' teams. Because of this the leader should prepare very carefully before the launch, focusing on each of the subjects discussed in this chapter and using or amending the practical methods for dealing with them that have been suggested here.

PROCESS REVIEW

Most of the problems faced by groups are to do with a failure to manage the dynamics of the group, or process, successfully. Because of this it is always necessary to have available a way of sharing and discussing perceptions about what is affecting the group in the way that it is working. In a conventional group this would normally take the form of a short discussion at the end of the meeting where everyone plays a part in analyzing what has happened in the meeting, learning from it and agreeing improvement objectives. This, of course, is not so easy when working in a 'virtual' team, but the vital importance of managing the group's process cannot be overstated.

The most effective way of handling this is for the leader to establish from the outset that there will be regular process reviews that everyone will be expected to contribute to. They should be scheduled from the start to take place either every week or every two weeks, depending on the intensity of the project, so that they become a normal part of the working of the team. It is a big mistake to conduct process reviews only when there is a problem since this will tend to lead to blame and recrimination rather than constructive discussion, understanding and improvement. The format of such 'virtual' reviews can vary but the ground rules need to be made clear from the start. Important amongst these are that:

O   everyone must take part and must put their name to their own comments

O   only process points are allowed, that is, things about the way the group and its members are working, not what they are working on

O   comments should be descriptive rather than judgemental

O   comments should be encouraged about what the group is doing successfully as well as things that seem to be holding it back

O   the process should culminate in an improvement plan.

So that individuals have the opportunity to discuss the points being made it is best to conduct the reviews in an online meeting.

ORGANIZATION CULTURE

As the use of 'virtual' teams becomes more common and widespread it is important for organizations that need or want to use this method to understand what they can do to help these activities to be successful. There is one main aspect of this; it is simple to describe but neither easy to implement nor to institutionalize. The organization needs to appreciate the demands and complexities involved in working in 'virtual' teams. For example, as well as the factors already covered in this chapter, the obvious issue of time differences when working globally will usually mean that members become involved in working 'anti-social' hours, unseen and often unnoticed by the organization at large, on issues that are not even within the framework of their 'day job'. The key issue then is one of recognition. Every organization that wishes to have motivated and committed people working in this way needs a recognition process. There are many possible ways of structuring this and it is important that a suitable scheme is designed for the people involved. Key features, however, should always include that the process is a public one so those receiving the accolade can not only see it themselves but can also see that others in the organization are equally aware. The recognition should be, in some sense, tangible but should not include money.

Finally it needs to be stated that virtual teams can be very powerful and effective, however there are certain types of problem or issue that are not conducive to this manner of working. If possible, set up a more conventional group if the issue:

- is volatile
- is iterative by its nature
- contains significant interpersonal issues
- requires high levels of creativity
- has significant 'political' implications
- is very urgent.

If there is no choice but to use this method in these circumstances, be very careful.

SUGGESTED AGENDA FOR AN INITIAL MEETING

Such a meeting is best organized over two days which will not only allow the group to cover a lot of ground, it will also enable people to meet socially which is an invaluable part of the team- and trust-building process. I would strongly suggest that a skilled facilitator is employed to help with the running of such meetings.

A typical agenda would cover the following:

- individual introductions
- introduction to the task (by the sponsor)
- agreement on group norms
- clarification and agreement on the task and goals of the group
- agreement on rules and procedures to be employed by the group including managing real and elapsed time
- sharing of Belbin team roles and discussion of implications for the group
- agreement on key roles within the group including technical roles required
- agreement on communication processes to be used
- agreement on method for process review
- summary of agreements
- statements of individual commitment.

Note:

- There should be a process review at the end of each of these segments.
- Repetition and reinforcement should be built into the agenda.

○   The expression of residual doubts should be encouraged at all times.

○   Virtual teams beware!

SUMMARY

Virtual teams are here to stay, of that there is no doubt. As time goes by we will learn more precisely what is required for them to be fully effective, but even now we know that the issues that have been covered in this chapter are essential ingredients.

PART II
PROBLEM-SOLVING TECHNIQUES

❖

5

THE PROBLEM-SOLVING PROCESS

❖

There's more than one way to skin a cat.

Having looked at the structure and composition of the different types of problem-solving group and also how they operate, we can turn our attention to the question of how they become effective. One of the main reasons that such groups so often fail, or at least their performance is less than expected, is that far too many assumptions are made about the level of skill that people have, both in solving problems in an organized way and also in working together successfully. The reality is that very few people have a natural talent for both of these elements, and so a careful and comprehensive training process will usually be required to equip both leaders and members of the planned groups, based on the tools and techniques described here. In addition, many organizations are today beginning to realize the power of using trained facilitators to assist groups in their work. The role of the facilitator is described in Chapter 17.

TRAINING

The training that is required can be organized in a number of different ways depending on the preferred style of those involved. For some, reading this book followed by the ability to practise the techniques in a group will be enough, whereas for others more formal training is required. In this event, a programme should be devised that enables attendees not only to learn the theory of the techniques, but also to practise them. Experience dictates that probably the best approach is to train leaders and facilitators using a formal training programme, and to teach group members during the course of the problem-solving meetings, on a need-to-know basis. This means that people are given the opportunity of using the techniques to address real issues immediately after they have been trained. This provides excellent reinforcement and means that the techniques are more likely to be retained. We remember 10 per cent of what we hear, 50 per cent of what we see and 80 per cent of what we do, so this last method is technically the most likely to succeed. So a knowledge of the problem-solving process and the main issues in working together successfully are important if we are going to achieve actual results and avoid just talking around subjects.

ANALYTICAL AND CREATIVE THINKING

What then is the problem-solving process, and which techniques are used in it? The problem-solving process needs to be rigorous, and for this it needs to combine both analytical and creative approaches. The analytical method will ensure that the issue to be addressed is clearly defined at the outset, and that the analysis and solution are based on fact rather than opinion. These are essential ingredients, but are not entirely sufficient since pure analytical thinking depends entirely on rationality and will not countenance apparently irrational or unconventional possibilities. Many problems are not new. They have been tackled before in an analytical way, but they returned, leaving us with the need for new solutions to old problems.

Pure analytical thinking is rather like a treadmill; it drives us round and round the same route. In a static world this may be enough, but in a world that is turbulent and ever changing it cannot be sufficient, which is why there is a need for creative techniques within the problem-solving process. Do not think that this will weaken the structure; we should be reminded that in the higher echelons of science, for example, mathematics and physics, progress is almost entirely conceptual and creative. Einstein, for example, had an unconventional creative thought whilst riding his bicycle on the road which led up to the town hall. He noticed the clock and, almost in an instant, developed the Theory of Relativity. After this amazing insight he went back to his desk and started trying to prove it mathematically.

STEPS IN THE PROBLEM-SOLVING PROCESS

This book combines both analytical and creative techniques into a coherent and powerful approach to problem-solving in groups. The main steps of the process are:

O   brainstorming
O   defining the problem clearly
O   analyzing the problem
O   collecting data
O   interpreting the data
O   generating possible solutions
O   agreeing the best solutions
O   cost-benefit analysis
O   presenting solutions
O   implementing solutions
O   monitoring and evaluating.

Within these steps a range of practical, fundamental techniques are used to help the group move from one stage to the next. These are covered in detail later but it will be useful to overview them here.

THE MAIN TECHNIQUES

BRAINSTORMING

Brainstorming is the core creative technique used by groups. It is very useful for helping people generate a large number of ideas in a short space of time and ensures that everyone contributes. Brainstorming is a well-known but often badly practised technique, and it is important that problem-solving groups learn to use it properly since all too often so-called brainstorming sessions involve no more than making lists of the obvious possibilities. Many other creative techniques are developments from, or variations on, brainstorming and these different techniques can be used at various stages of the problem-solving process. The rules of brainstorming are explained in detail in Chapter 6, together with the recommended procedure for using it.

DEFINING PROBLEMS

Many groups founder because they pay too little attention to defining the real problem. Often so-called problem statements are actually thinly disguised solutions. For example, 'The problem is that we need a new kitchen'! On other occasions groups simply end up tackling the wrong issue because of the assumptions they make at the outset. Groups need a mechanism to enable them to avoid these difficulties at the start of the process. 'Occam's Razor', a technique to help groups arrive at a precisely defined problem statement, is discussed in Chapter 7.

ANALYZING PROBLEMS

Chapter 8 looks at the two methods of analysis which have been found most suitable for dealing with the types of problem that groups tackle. The techniques are called Fishbone Analysis and the Six-Word Diagram. Fishbone diagrams were first developed in Japan by Ishikawa who was the father of the development of employee participation in his country. They are often called Ishikawa Diagrams, or Cause and Effect Diagrams. The Six-Word Diagram was developed by Mike Robson in 1980 to assist groups to analyze problems that were not amenable to Fishbone Analysis.

COLLECTING DATA

One of the most important things for groups to do if they are to achieve success is to present their arguments in terms of facts rather than opinions. This inevitably leads to the requirement to collect information about the present situation. Chapter 9 explains why it is important to collect the facts and describes the most common mechanisms used by problem-solving groups to do this. Since one of the most common failings of groups is to rely on their opinions rather than facts, this is a critical stage in the whole process and simple techniques are needed to assist the group.

INTERPRETING DATA

The best way of interpreting the data will vary but a number of key tools will always be useful. As a general rule, interpreting data is made easier if the numbers are put into a visual form, so graphs are a useful aid. Chapter 10 looks at some of the most widely used methods of interpreting data including Pareto charts and histograms which are useful aids to understanding. These two mechanisms are important because they help to reveal patterns in the data, whether it be the most important issue or the distribution.

FINDING SOLUTIONS

On the basis of the data collected, the group will need to generate possible solutions and to establish the costs and benefits as a part of deciding the best way forward. Force-field analysis is one powerful technique to use at this stage, and so are the Delphi, the solutions fishbone diagram, swapping and collages. All these techniques are useful in different circumstances, depending on whether a really creative solution is required, whether the problem is concerned with people or objects, or whether a more analytically based solution will be most appropriate. The range of techniques and the procedure for using them are discussed in detail in Chapter 11.

COST-BENEFIT ANALYSIS

Once a provisional solution has been arrived at it needs to be carefully evaluated. Often the solution proposed will involve a cost or investment – the purchase of new equipment perhaps. The group must consider whether the extra outlay will be justified – will the rewards outweigh the expenditure?

Costs and benefits can be compared systematically by means of a technique called – not surprisingly – Cost-Benefit Analysis. This is examined in Chapter 12.

PRESENTING SOLUTIONS

The normal outcome of the problem-solving process is that the group presents its recommendations to management for decision. Obviously groups will be keen to present their solutions in as positive a way as possible to give themselves the maximum chance of success. Chapter 13 describes how to make management presentations, including techniques that are invaluable in helping groups to sell their solutions. This chapter provides a structure to work through and guidelines for preparing, rehearsing and delivering the presentation.

MONITORING AND EVALUATION

Good solutions often fail as a result of the variety of problems that can get in the way of successful implementation. A monitoring and evaluating system is an essential part of the problem-solving process to ensure that the anticipated benefits are achieved and also that the problem does not return once the focus has been switched elsewhere. This subject is covered in more detail in Chapter 14.

There is no doubt that groups need a rigorous process with practical tools and techniques if they are to be successful, but many groups make the mistake of thinking that this is all that is required to ensure success. Unfortunately it is not. Just as essential as the problem-solving techniques is that the group functions effectively in its work. Camels may be horses designed by committees, but only when the group is ineffective in the way it works. Managed properly, group working can be very powerful and is an important part of any organizational improvement process.

STATE OF MIND

The state of mind that group members adopt as they approach the problem is a key part of the overall process recommended in this book. It may seem strange to include this in a chapter on problem-solving, but in fact it is at least as important as the problem-solving steps themselves, for a number of reasons.

ASSUMPTIONS

First, the nature of the problem is very much influenced by our state of mind. The following story illustrates this point. A man whose lawn-mower broke down while he was cutting the grass at home went indoors to speak to his wife about it and she suggested that he called next door and asked their neighbour if he could borrow his. It seemed like a sensible idea, and so he went to the door. Just as he reached it a thought occurred to him, 'What if the neighbour refuses?' He opened the door and went out. Halfway down the path another thought struck him: 'Last year when I needed a spade to dig the garden, the neighbour lent it to me but he didn't seem all that pleased.' By the time he got to the gate he was thinking, 'He might be planning to cut his own lawn this afternoon.' As he walked down the neighbour's drive, the thoughts flooded through his brain. 'If he's planning to do his own lawn he would have to say "no". Anyway, he might be worried that I would break the machine so that he wouldn't be able to cut his lawn tomorrow.' By the time he reached his neighbour's door he was thinking, 'I never did like this bloke – he wouldn't lend his lawn-mower to his best friend, there's no way he would lend it to me.' He knocked on the door, and as soon as his neighbour opened it, he said, 'And you know what you can do with your lawn-mower!'

This story illustrates how very dangerous it can be to make assumptions about the way other people are thinking. Wherever possible, we should be well advised in our meetings to avoid assuming things about people and their motives and concentrate on solving our own problems.

FINGER-POINTING

Our state of mind also concerns finger-pointing – or, 'it's your fault'. Finger-pointing happens all the time, but never achieves anything. It is worth remembering that for every finger that we point, there are at least three pointing back at us. If we are saying, 'it's all their fault', it is a sure bet that they are saying it is all ours. It is important to recognize with finger-pointing that it does not matter who is right or wrong; if they think we are at fault, then it is 'true' as far as they are concerned, just as much as we think it is 'true' that they are to blame. This is why finger-pointing has no place in group working; all it does is lead to frustration, it never helps things to get better. One problem, of course, is that it is very easy to revert to this habit, so we help ourselves and our colleagues by reminding each other if we do lapse.

FOCUS ON THE PROBLEM

The third consideration, as far as our state of mind is concerned, is to do with whose problems we are trying to solve. This, in some ways, is linked to finger-pointing. One of the most important guidelines to ensure successful group working is to remember that we should concentrate on what we can achieve, and not pass the buck. One of the most important reasons why problem-solving groups are so successful is that they concentrate on the problems that they have been given – those they can do something about.

WIN/WIN

Finally, as far as our state of mind is concerned, it is important to recognize that we are trying to create a situation where everyone wins.

In summary, then, the four problem-solving states of mind are:

O   Avoid making assumptions about what others are thinking.
O   Do not blame anyone or any other department.
O   Concentrate on what has been asked to be achieved and do not pass the buck.
O   Build a situation where everyone wins.

Problem-solving groups are not there to do anyone down, to beat anyone or to show people up. They are there to solve problems, to make their members' working lives more satisfactory and enjoyable, and to enable them to contribute their skill and experience to help their organization survive and succeed.

SUMMARY

To solve problems effectively there is an obvious need for a disciplined approach that uses organized and proven techniques which assist the group in its work. This alone, however, is not enough. Many groups use good problem-solving techniques but fail because they do not work effectively together. This book is unique in bringing together the aspects of the problem-solving process with its techniques and also the issues involved in working together.

6

BRAINSTORMING

The best way to have a good idea is to have lots of ideas.

This chapter concentrates on a technique known as brainstorming, which is used extensively by problem-solving groups at various stages of their activities. Brainstorming was developed in the 1930s by Alex Osborne as a way of encouraging groups to be more creative in their ideas. But before we go through the procedures and rules of brainstorming, it will be useful to look at the quite different kinds of thinking that members can use in their group work.

ANALYTICAL THINKING

The first of these is analytical thinking. Most people have fairly highly developed skills in this area (for example, in mathematics and the other sciences), which is not surprising since our schooling focuses on developing analytical skills and the workplace reinforces them. As such most of us, when presented with a problem, will tackle it in an analytical way.

LATERAL THINKING

Other problems require a strictly analytical approach but with a measure of creativity to give the insight needed to get on the right wavelength. This kind of insight is sometimes called lateral thinking.

CREATIVE THINKING

There are yet other types of question where there is no one right answer, and it is helpful to have many different ideas and thoughts about it before making up our mind, in other words, to think creatively. Some examples of such questions are:

O   How can the company sell more of its products?
O   Where shall I go for my holiday this year?
O   How can we reduce the number of road accidents?

Many of the kinds of problems that problem-solving groups tackle require a creative approach to ensure that every possibility is explored in arriving at the preferred solution. Questions such as:

O   How can we improve quality in our department?
O   How can we reduce waste?
O   How can we make sure that everyone is better trained?

Although problems like these are the kind that will respond to being tackled creatively, this is not to say that problem-solving groups do not use analytical problem-solving skills; they do. However, they also use creative techniques which give their solutions originality and freshness.

BARRIERS TO CREATIVITY

Just as we are brought up to be good at analytical thinking, there is much in the average upbringing that hinders real creative thought, and it is important that we recognize the main types of barrier to creativity before we move on to look in detail at the technique of brainstorming.

TRAMLINE THINKING

The first – and one of the most important – barriers to creative thought is the tendency to assume that the way things have always been done is the only way they can be done and to limit our thinking to the boundaries of our present experience. The problem of precedence is that we limit our thoughts by making assumptions about what is possible. How often do we hear people say: 'Yes, but we've always done it like that!'

FEAR OF LOOKING FOOLISH

The second barrier to creative thought is the fear of looking foolish. Many of us will remember how we refrained from asking questions at school because nobody else was and we therefore assumed that they knew what the teacher was talking about. Later, sometimes years later, we realized that everyone was avoiding asking questions for just the same reason, the fear of being ridiculed by our classmates! This tendency limits our contributions to things that are safe and conventional. It very often prevents our coming up with an unconventional suggestion which would either be exactly right or could spark off a good idea in someone else.

INSTANT EVALUATION

The third barrier is our tendency to evaluate instantaneously. How many times do ideas get thrown into the waste bin without anyone really giving them a chance and 'trying them on for size', because at first they appear impractical, impossible or simply crazy?

ONE RIGHT ANSWER

The final barrier to creative thought is the commonly held view that there is one right answer to every problem. This tends to drive people immediately into an analytical thinking mode and to look for the single obvious and logical answer. This is fine when there is one, but often there is not, and this barrier prevents people from looking for the less obvious, creative solution.

Alex Osborne realized that it was these barriers which blocked the flow of creative ideas and proposed the rules of brainstorming as a way of overcoming the barriers, not for all time, but for a short period of 20–30 minutes. He reasoned that it was unlikely that most people would really be able to change the habits of a lifetime but that given a framework we could all hold back the barriers for a short period of time and allow our underlying creativity to pour out.

RULES OF BRAINSTORMING

There is little doubt that the driving force behind the creativity of problem-solving groups is the technique of brainstorming, and we can move on now to look at it in more detail. Brainstorming is a method of getting a group of people to generate many ideas in a short space of time. It sounds easy, but in fact it requires much practice for most groups to become proficient at it. Once the groups do master the technique, however, it becomes an invaluable tool in their problem-solving kit.

RULE 1: NO CRITICISM

The first rule of brainstorming is that there should be no criticism of any ideas thrown up during the meeting. This is essential if we are to overcome the barriers talked about earlier. The 'no criticism' rule involves trying to suspend judgement of ideas and suggestions until after the brainstorming meeting. This is, in fact, much easier to say than to do, since most of us tend to be very judgemental. To be really effective the 'no criticism' rule should apply not only to what we say. Body language can be devastatingly negative and critical so this has to be watched. Furthermore, criticism of what we are thinking, self-censorship, is perhaps the biggest criticism of all. They are all a part of the 'no criticism' rule.

RULE 2: FREEWHEELING

The second rule of brainstorming is freewheeling. It is widely accepted that we have many of our creative ideas when our brainwaves are in the so-called theta pattern. This occurs when we are just dropping off to sleep, just waking up, driving on a long journey and so on, times at which our mind roams free. It is this state that we should try to get into whilst brainstorming. As such, the freewheeling rule encourages us to come up with random ideas off the top of our heads. It does not matter how apparently impractical the ideas are; in fact, brainstorming meetings are much more effective if crazy ideas are really encouraged. In some brainstorming meetings, it is worth spending a few minutes concentrating on listing the most ludicrous ideas possible concerning the subject in hand.

RULE 3: QUANTITY

The third rule is to generate as many ideas as possible. Brainstorming is very much about quantity rather than quality in the first instance. To help ensure that the maximum number of ideas are put forward, it is useful to get into the habit of thinking around ideas as they are given and using them as a springboard for further possibilities. Building on what is already there is a vital part of a successful brainstorming meeting. Typically groups will aim at producing 100 ideas in 20 minutes, though even this is a modest target if the brainstorming meeting is going really well since lists of well over 250 ideas can be achieved in a 20 minute period.

RULE 4: RECORD ALL IDEAS

The fourth rule is that each idea must be written down, however extraordinary it may seem, and even if it is the same as a previous idea but expressed in a different way. Furthermore, this must be done in such a way that the whole group can see the list as it is being compiled. The scribe needs to write the ideas on a flip chart and, when full, the sheets need to be posted around the room so that they remain in view and therefore can be referred to and used by group members. Brainstorming meetings are supposed to be fast and furious, and it is often difficult to hear all the ideas being put forward, let alone get them all down, and so it should be the responsibility of the other members to make sure that all ideas are recorded, by repeating themselves where necessary. So that the pace of the meeting can be kept up it is useful for the scribe to abbreviate ideas as much as possible, obviously taking care not to change the content of the suggestion.

RULE 5: INCUBATE

The fifth rule of brainstorming is to incubate the ideas before evaluating them. This process ensures that we do not judge ideas before we have had the chance really to think about them. Problem-solving groups usually incubate their brainstorming meetings for a week and come back to their lists at the next group meeting with a further few minutes of brainstorming to see if any more ideas have occurred to anyone during the week.

SUMMARY

To summarize, the rules of brainstorming are:

1   There should be no criticism of any idea.
2   Freewheeling is encouraged.
3   Concentrate on getting the maximum number of ideas.
4   Record every idea, even repetition.
5   Incubate all the ideas, do not reject anything out of hand.

A BRAINSTORMING MEETING

Having dealt with the rules of brainstorming, we can now turn our attention to the steps in running a successful brainstorming meeting and evaluating the ideas after they have been incubated.

STEP 1

The first step for a successful meeting is to restate and write up the rules of brainstorming. In posting the list of rules on a wall so that everyone can see it, members are reminded of them during the meeting and can make sure that they adhere to them. Always do this; it is easy to assume that everyone will be able to slot easily into the process – they won't!

STEP 2

This is to write up the subject to be brainstormed. This is usually best done by preceding it with the phrase, 'What are all the ways we can … ?' So, at an initial brainstorming meeting for generating a list of possible problems to work on, a group might write up, 'What are all the ways we can improve our department?' Later on in the problem-solving cycle, the heading might be, 'What are all the ways we can reduce waste?' Writing the headings up in this way helps to make sure the group stays focused on the topic in hand.

STEP 3

The third step is to start the ideas coming. Some groups choose to do this by going round the room and taking it in turns to call out an idea. If anyone cannot think of a suggestion, he or she just says 'pass' and the next person carries on so that the flow of ideas is not halted. This way of organizing the meeting has the advantage of making sure that everyone is involved and that the ideas come one at a time, which makes it easier to record them.

Most brainstorming groups, however, seem to prefer the unstructured 'free-for-all' approach where anyone can call out an idea at any time. This method puts a greater strain on the person doing the writing, but probably results in a better quality of brainstorming, since ideas are really coming freely and naturally. Obviously with this approach it is not possible to make sure that everyone participates, but as groups develop their skill at using the technique this becomes less of a problem. This second approach is probably better, but both have their merits. Whichever method is used, people doing the job of scribe should play an active part in the process by calling out and recording their own ideas as well as those of the other members.

STEP 4

This is to record the ideas and to make sure that the full list is visible to the whole group all the time. It is not sufficient to write the ideas on a flip chart and then just turn the page over when it is full. With this in mind, a supply of masking tape or Blu Tak should be available to enable completed sheets to be posted somewhere on the walls.

STEP 5

This is to incubate the ideas. The best way of doing this is to post the lists somewhere in the work area. This has a number of advantages. It ensures that other people in the section, who are not in the group, can see what the group has been doing, and even contribute ideas of their own and add them to the lists should they so desire. The other benefit of posting the lists in the work area is that it keeps the subject in mind and this can help the incubation process.

STEP 6

The final step is to begin the process of evaluation. This is normally done in the following group meeting. The best way of organizing the evaluation is to begin by grouping the items on the list into themes. This should be done before any items are rejected as being impractical. Once the list has been rewritten into themes, the suggestions on each subject can be explored to identify instant winners, ideas that can be quickly and easily implemented.

What happens next in the problem-solving cycle depends on the subject of the brainstorming. If it was to find a problem to work on, the group would select a general theme and then focus attention on the ideas recorded under the heading to find a suitable issue with which they should deal. Alternatively, if the group had brainstormed possible solutions, the next step would be to look at the list of possibilities and use Pareto analysis, which is defined in Chapter 10, to isolate the one or two ideas that would solve most of the problem. The Pareto principle would also be used in scrutinizing the detailed ideas for precise solutions.

SUMMARY

The six steps in running a brainstorming meeting are as follows:

1   Write up the rules of brainstorming and post them on a wall.
2   Write up the subject to be brainstormed.
3   Start the ideas coming.
4   Record all the suggestions, however crazy.
5   Incubate the ideas.
6   Evaluate the ideas using the Pareto principle.

Brainstorming is one of the most important techniques used by problem-solving groups and one of the most enjoyable. It is designed to be fun, and experience shows that when groups are relaxed, they produce many more ideas. Since this is the idea of brainstorming, remember to enjoy it!

7

DEFINING PROBLEMS CLEARLY

If you don't know where you're going, you won't know when you get there!

Many problem-solvers, whether groups or individuals, seriously limit their effectiveness by failing to define the problem they are working on clearly enough.

DIFFERENT PERCEPTIONS

The main problem here is that members of problem-solving groups often have quite different perceptions about what they want to get out of the group in terms of solutions. An example of this was a group working on the problem they defined as 'poor working conditions'. They found that it was hard work dealing with this issue and it took them a long time to see that one of the problems was that they all had different 'hidden agendas'. Some of the group were looking to improve productivity through improving conditions, others were concerned only with safety issues, while yet others were concerned with reducing labour turnover or removing an obstacle to the forthcoming wage negotiations or simply making the company a better place in which to work in a general sense.

DISGUISED SOLUTION STATEMENTS

A second difficulty is that many so-called problem statements are actually thinly disguised solution statements. Examples here are any statements with the word 'more' or 'less' in them. People in organizations tend very often to think in terms of solutions – how often do we hear, 'what we need is … ', or 'what they should do is … '. The difficulty here is whether or not the proposed solution is in fact the correct one – it often is not.

An example of this comes from a department group which was convinced that the problem was, 'We need more space'. They agreed to work on a revised problem statement, however, having seen that more space was a solution, even though the members all thought it was the only answer. They redefined the problem as 'The work area is congested' and found that by using the problem-solving process in full they were able to solve the problem by a combination of improved housekeeping and a new storage system including racking. Furthermore, they saved so much space in doing this that they were able to free up a sizeable area which they converted to a meeting area.

GENERALIZED PROBLEM STATEMENTS

A third difficulty with problem statements is that they are often so broad and general that it is impossible for the group to get its minds round the issue and tackle it in anything other than a broad and general way. Problem-solving groups need to deal with practical issues that are capable of being resolved to the benefit of the organization and the people in it. Dealing with global issues like 'poor communication' or 'bad attitudes' is unlikely to facilitate this, and so these groups need a tool to help break down broad generalities into 'bite-sized chunks'. What is needed here is a technique that will assist in this important first step of any problem-solving process.

OCCAM'S RAZOR

William of Occam was born in England in 1280. He became a Franciscan monk and studied at Oxford University. He was a revolutionary philosopher and his work helped lay the foundations of modern theories of government. He is most famous for his dictum, *Entia non sunt multiplicando praeter necessitatem*, which means that beings ought not to be multiplied except out of necessity. Known as 'Occam's Razor', this statement has a wide application and is used today to suggest that things should be kept as simple and uncluttered as possible, and that we should keep to the core issue.

The 'Occam's Razor' technique can help both individuals and groups define their problems more clearly. It involves three steps.

STEP 1

This is to establish the broad problem area. Very often the problem to be tackled is chosen from a long list of issues which have been generated as the result of a brainstorming meeting. This is likely to be the case, for example, with improvement teams and issue teams, though with department groups and task forces the problem is given to the group, so this step may not be necessary. Where it is needed, however, there is a need for a way of getting at a suitable issue without having to consider every single idea in detail. The techniques used in these circumstances are called Theme Analysis and the Four Guidelines.

Theme Analysis

Theme Analysis simply involves reordering the random brainstorming list into broad categories or themes.

First the group should discuss and agree what are the main themes within their brainstorming list. Usually there will be between five and eight main categories and it is important to take care, in choosing the themes, that they really do reflect the ideas in the brainstorming. In Theme Analysis there will usually be a place for a category called 'other' to take the miscellaneous items that do not fit anywhere else. Having agreed the theme headings and checked that there is not too much overlap between them, the group is ready to allocate each idea from the brainstorming into one or other theme. There are two important points to be remembered in doing this. First, do not put ideas into more than one theme since this becomes very unwieldy. Second, have the group allocate ideas to themes quickly without dwelling on it too much. The quickest way of doing this is to number the themes and then go through the brainstorming list adding the number of the theme in a different colour. Having done this the lists should be rewritten under theme headings. This can be done by members during the meeting or by a volunteer between meetings. It is, however, important to rewrite the list to assist the group in the next stages of its work.

Having completed the Theme Analysis the next steps are to choose one of the themes to work on initially and then to choose one of the issues from within this theme as the problem to be tackled. There is a need for a simple technique at this stage, to ensure that the issue selected is an appropriate one.

The Four Guidelines

The recommended method is called the Four Guidelines. The purpose of the guidelines is to act as a sieve which will filter out any problems which it would be inappropriate to tackle. The guidelines take the form of questions as follows:

1   Is it in our own house? Here we are filtering out any issues which we cannot influence.
2   Can we do something about it in a reasonable time? For the most part we will want to deal with issues that we can influence in a period of weeks or months, rather than years.
3   Can we collect data about it? It is essential that problems are solved in terms of facts, not opinions, so we need to select issues where data can be collected.
4   Do we really want to solve it? Especially for problems that will be tackled by groups it is important that everyone actively wants to tackle the issue.

The group needs to use these guidelines rigorously to sort out inappropriate choices. The Four Guidelines are used twice in doing this. The first step is to post the theme headings on the wall and use the Four Guidelines in choosing one theme to focus on. Having done this, the ideas contained in the chosen theme are posted and the guidelines are used again to select the particular issue or group of issues on which the group wants initially to focus. Careful use of these guidelines will result in the selection of a suitable problem area. At this stage, however, it will not necessarily be defined clearly enough or worded precisely enough.

STEP 2

Having agreed the problem area, Step 2 involves helping the group to get back to the core issue. A trap that many individuals and groups fall into is not paying enough attention to the precise definition of the problem, and often in groups the impatience of some of the members can result in this stage being missed out completely. This step is important for task forces and department groups even though they have been given their problem, since the statement may not be worded precisely enough. There are three steps involved at this point:

1   The initial problem statement should be written on a flip chart and posted somewhere visible.
2   Each member of the group should be given some paper or a supply of 20 x 13 cms cards and a pen.

3   Members of the group should now be asked to consider the problem statement carefully. It should be explained to group members that often problem statements are actually disguised solution statements. Examples should be given to the group, such as:

○   'We need more space.'
○   'We need a new machine.'
○   'We need to update our computer system.'

All these are possible solutions to a problem. They may not be the correct solution, however, and so we need to get back to the core problem. Group members should be asked to consider the initial problem statement carefully and ask whether it is a solution statement in disguise. Words to look out for here include 'more', 'less', 'improved' and so on, since they indicate a possible solution statement. If this is the case in the group's view, members should be asked to think of the statement and to answer the question: 'What is the main problem that would be solved if we had ... [specify from problem statement]?' So, for example, if the problem statement was 'We need more space', the group would be asked, 'What is the main problem that would be solved if we had more space?' Individual members should write their thoughts down on the cards provided.

4   Next the members should be invited to display the cards and to group all their answers into categories, with any similar or duplicated ideas being pulled together within the same category.

5   Having reached this point, the group is in a position to discuss the real underlying problem that it wishes to tackle. It is important to note that this will not necessarily be the issue with the most cards, so members should discuss each possibility and come to a genuine consensus.

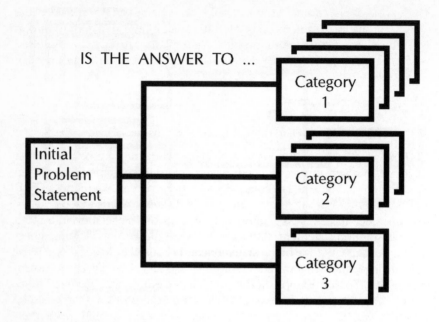

It is possible of course that the problem statement as defined initially does not conceal an assumed solution, in which case the group will have decided not to go through this exercise. In this event the group should consider whether or not the statement that they have is specific enough to work on usefully. Problem statements like 'bad communications', 'poor management' or 'employee attitudes' are very broad and will be difficult to tackle in an overall sense. If the group feels that their statement comes in this category, members should address this using a procedure similar to the one outlined above, but this time the question that everyone answers individually is, 'What is the main problem that ... causes in our organization?' So in the case of 'bad communications' the question would be, 'What is the main problem that bad communications causes in our organization?' Having done this, the ideas are revealed and grouped as before. Once this has been done the group is in a position to discuss which of the statements is the real problem the group wishes to focus on. This again need not be the problem with the most 'votes'.

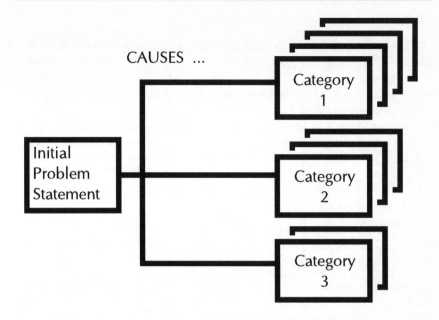

So far we have dealt with a way of handling problem statements that are actually solutions and ones that are too generalized to be able to work on usefully. The third aspect of problem statements that needs to be addressed relates to group members' perceptions of what they want from the solution to the problem. Again the process is similar. The problem statement should be written up and posted somewhere visible. Next, each individual member should write on a card what he or she would like to see as the outcome of the problem-solving process in relation to this problem. Again the ideas are shared and grouped, and at this stage the group can discuss whether or not an amendment to the problem statement is needed, either to make it clearer or to reflect a different balance or perspective.

Step 2, in applying 'Occam's Razor' thus involves the group considering its existing problem statement and using whichever of the three methods that have been outlined to ensure that they agree a definition that everyone understands and is committed to, and that really does identify the core issue at hand. The three methods address:

○   problems expressed as solutions
○   problem statements that are too general
○   members having different reasons for addressing the problem.

Not every method will be used every time. The group should decide on what is appropriate, though experience shows that the third tool is worth building into the early stages of every problem-solving group.

STEP 3

Having got this far, the third and final step in this technique is to ask the question, 'So what?' The group should discuss this seriously with a view to agreeing whether or not focusing on this issue will be a good use of time, since there is little point in proceeding if the group actually feels that the problem is not worth tackling.

Assuming that it is agreed to be worthwhile, the full problem statement should be recorded on a flip chart and displayed during every meeting, to act as a constant reminder to the team of the precise nature of its endeavours.

The three steps involved in defining the problem clearly using 'Occam's Razor' are therefore:

1   Establish the broad problem area.
2   Get back to the core issue and agree the precise problem statement.
3   Ask if this problem is worth tackling.

Having problems examined in this way helps to ensure that activities remain focused and that groups are channelling their energies to the analysis and solution of the precise issue that concerns them. Remember, if you don't know where you are going, you won't know when you arrive!

SUMMARY

Getting the right answer to the wrong question is probably the most common cause of failure in problem-solving, whether individually or in groups, so it is vitally important that sound techniques are used to be precise about the issue at hand.

8

ANALYZING PROBLEMS

For now we see through a glass, darkly. (1 Corinthians XIII v. 11)

This chapter deals with the recommended methods for problem-solving groups to use in analyzing the problems they tackle. Many of the problems faced by organizations appear at first glance to be simple to solve, but, as groups soon find out, this is very rarely the case. The reason for this is that there is not usually a unique solution that everyone agrees is right. What might seem perfectly obvious from one point of view, is often far from obvious to someone else. Problem-solving groups are effective for many reasons, but none more important than this: that they explore all the possible solutions to the problem. This willingness to see a problem from different perspectives from their own adds considerably to the practicality of the solutions they propose, and helps in overcoming the biggest potential hurdle to successful implementation, namely that of people's attitude at all levels of the organization. So often a good solution does not work in practice because no one owns it or some have been alienated from it.

WIN/WIN

We have said before that these groups are all about everybody winning, and it is a point worthy of constant repetition. If an unhealthy win/lose situation does develop, it is remarkable how often the losers can make the cost of winning very high, thus turning a win/lose situation into one in which everyone loses. The fact that most organizational problems have more than one cause, and are capable of being solved in more than one way, suggests that the methods used for analyzing the problems should encourage creative as well as analytical thought, and the techniques covered in this chapter fulfil both criteria.

REAL CAUSES

Whichever method is used, this stage in the problem-solving cycle is crucial to success. One of the major reasons for failures to solve problems is a wrong diagnosis of the real causes. It may seem trite to say so, but devising a brilliant solution to the wrong cause is unlikely to get the group very far. Obvious though this may be, there are countless examples of individuals and groups who have fallen into this trap. The usual reason for this is that people often tend only to look at problems from the standpoint of the seemingly obvious causes and do not look at the problem from all sides before coming to a view. Often the factors which are commonly assumed to be causes turn out on analysis to be only symptoms.

THINK BROADLY

The really successful problem-solving groups are those which do not readily accept the apparently obvious answer and insist on trying to think all the way round the problem.

With any problem, the more alternatives the group considers, the better will be the solution that it eventually decides on, and to have members of the group actively thinking of new alternatives can greatly assist the process. One of the difficulties in working in a problem-solving group is that members sometimes tend to go along with the majority rather than actively try to think of new ways of looking at the problem. The reason for using organized techniques that encourage creative thinking is that it helps to give members the confidence to contribute unusual ideas and suggestions.

THE MAIN TECHNIQUES

Fishbone and Six-Word Diagrams are just two of the many possible methods of analysis. Groups need to decide on the appropriate method depending on the precise nature of the problem in hand. Sometimes the group may believe it to be more appropriate simply to talk through the problem informally and to record main points on a flip chart as the discussion progresses. Where this is the case, however, the group needs to be sure that it looks at the situation from all angles and that it is not taking too narrow a view. The techniques covered in this section force this wider perspective.

THE FISHBONE DIAGRAM

The first, and probably most common, method of analyzing problems used by problem-solving groups is the Fishbone Diagram, otherwise known as the Cause and Effect Diagram. It is called a Fishbone Diagram because its structure resembles the skeleton of a fish. Fishbone Diagrams are a means of separating causes from effects and are of great assistance to these groups in seeing a problem in its totality. Many problems take on a different perspective when viewed in this way. Causes which previously seemed to be central often fade in importance as the group's analysis brings other key causes to light.

There are six steps in the construction of a Fishbone Diagram.

Step 1

The first step is to write up the effect on the right-hand side of a large sheet of paper. It is important at this stage to ensure that the effect chosen by the group is as precise as possible. The more general the effect, the more general will be the causes, and this often makes it difficult to get to grips with the problem. Problem-solving groups are concerned with actually getting things done rather than talking about them in vague and general terms, so they do need to get down to identifying the detailed causes of the problem, which requires that the effect is defined in as clear and specific a way as possible.

It may be useful to give some examples. Effects such as 'poor quality', or 'bad working conditions' are very broad and are more suited to being a general theme for the group to work on, rather than the precise problem within the theme. Effects such as 'the high number of revised drawings circulated' or 'the cramped office layout', are more specific and likely to lead to a more useful Fishbone Diagram.

Step 2

The second step is to draw in the main ribs of the fish, and to write in the headings of the main problem areas. Experience shows that six headings are adequate for the majority of situations encountered, and all six headings should be included on the sheet:

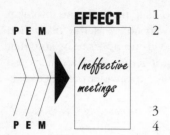

1   **P**eople and everything to do with them.

2   **E**nvironment in which the work is conducted, including heat, cold, draughts, sitting and standing positions and many other aspects of working conditions.

3   **M**ethods employed to do the work.

4   **P**lant, which includes such items as the machinery, computers, the boiler house and the buildings themselves.

5   **E**quipment, such as tools, overalls, stationery, filing cabinets, and so on

6   **M**aterials used to do the job.

You may have noticed that the first letters of the headings spell out PEMPEM, which is a useful memory jogger. It is worth noting at this point that there may well be instances where not all of the headings are relevant or where additional headings are needed. In these circumstances the group can add to or delete the number of ribs. Care must be taken, of course, only to add ribs that are broad areas of cause. For example, with some problems the heading 'Communication' may be needed.

Step 3

The next step in constructing the diagram is for the group to remind itself of the rules of brainstorming (see Chapter 6) and to write them up somewhere so that everyone can see them.

Step 4

This is to use the rules and procedures of brainstorming to generate the list of causes which relate to the effect which has been written down. It is at this point in the proceedings that the person doing the writing needs to concentrate on getting the ideas up on the diagram in the right place, since members will be calling out ideas to do with all six headings. It is not only a matter of placing suggestions under the most obvious headings though.

Let us focus attention for a minute on just one part of the 'Incorrect' diagram.

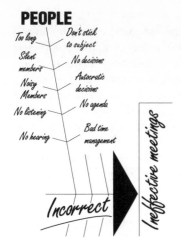

If a Fishbone Diagram ends up looking like this, it does not make the best use of the technique. This is because it does not indicate the real linkages between the different causes and leaves the group with a further job of grouping causes after the diagram has been completed. Some suggestions spring from, and build on, other ideas and can best be expressed as a branch of a previous cause. The 'Correct' diagram contains the same entries as the previous one but 'No listening' and 'No decisions' are seen as branches off the 'Don't stick to subject' line, and 'No hearing' and 'Autocratic decisions' are sub-branches of these. This gives a much clearer indication of the major groups of ideas for the group to work on, and is therefore more useful.

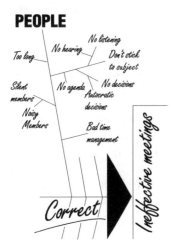

Help the scribe Two further points are important about this stage of work. The first is that group members can be of great assistance to the scribe, by indicating which of the six headings they think their suggestions should be recorded under, and the second is that any apparent repetition of ideas should still be recorded, especially if they are placed on a different part of the diagram. We have already said that organizational problems usually have many different causes and it is quite understandable, even likely, that the same cause of a particular problem can be analyzed under different headings.

Throughout this stage of completing the Fishbone Diagram, it is important that group members remember that they are responsible for seeing that their own suggestions and all the ideas of other members of the group are recorded on the diagram. This will ensure that they end up with the best possible basis for moving on to the next stage of the problem-solving process.

Step 5

The next step in the procedure is usually to incubate the ideas on the diagram for a while, to let them sink in and to ensure that none of the suggestions is rejected out of hand. This can be done either by sitting quietly for 10 minutes thinking about the implications of the completed diagram, or by posting the sheet up in the workplace between group meetings and thinking about it during the week. Of these two options, the second is preferable, not only because it gives more time to incubate, but also because it gives other people in the organization, who are not group members, a chance to see the output and to contribute to it if they so desire.

It is usually valuable and important that the group makes sure that others feel free to add to the work. Problem-solving groups are not exclusive clubs, and unless there are good reasons otherwise, such as confidentiality, it makes sense to give non-members the chance to contribute, especially if they may be involved in the implementation of any changes.

Step 6

This is to analyze the whole diagram. Here the group should look at the analysis and see which ideas and groups of ideas 'jump off the page'. The Pareto principle states that a few causes are likely to account for most of the effect, and it is these few causes that the group is looking for at this stage. At this point, the group has not collected data and is using its knowledge and experience to determine which are the essential areas to focus on as far as data collection is concerned.

Suppose that we believe the really important keys to improving the effectiveness of meetings are 'agendas' and 'time management'. In this case we would put a ring round these two causes and would be able to focus our data collection on these issues to see the extent to which they were really the underlying keys to success.

This, then, is the procedure for completing a Fishbone or Cause and Effect Diagram.

In summary the steps are:

1   Define the effect carefully and write it up.
2   Decide on the main problem headings and draw in the main ribs.
3   Review the rules of brainstorming and post them up.
4   Brainstorm the causes and write them up in the appropriate place.
5   Incubate the suggestions on the diagram.
6   Use the Pareto principle to estimate the main causes that the group needs to collect data about.

Cause and Effect Diagrams are one of the most important and widely used problem-analysis methods employed by problem-solving groups. They represent a useful blend of analytical and creative thought, and many solutions have come out of an insight which has stemmed from analyzing such a diagram.

THE SIX-WORD DIAGRAM

The second method of analysis, which sometimes fits the problem better, is a technique called the Six Honest Serving-Men or Six-Word Diagram. The title comes from a poem by Rudyard Kipling which talks about the value of the words 'What', 'Why', 'When', 'How', 'Where' and 'Who'.

These six words are essential to ensure that all the relevant questions are asked about any particular situation, and this is why the Six-Word Diagram is so powerful. The technique analyzes a problem or a desired state by using the words, in turn, to brainstorm its different dimensions. More than this, though, it encourages the group to look at the 'not problem' as well as the difficulty itself. For example, it asks the question, 'When does the problem not happen?' as well as 'When does the problem happen?' It is often just as productive to analyze the 'not problem' and this helps to ensure that the group really does look at the issue from every angle.

There are six steps in the construction of a Six-Word Diagram.

Step 1

The first is to define the problem precisely and to prepare for the meeting. This involves using 12 sheets of flip-chart paper since the technique is based on holding brainstorming sessions around 12 questions. It is important that the definition is clear and concise, and the main reason for this is worth repeating – that the more generalized the definition of the problem, the more generalized will be the analysis, and the higher the likelihood that the group will get bogged down in woolly concepts rather than real practicalities.

Step 2

This is to use the definition of the problem to assist in specifying the 12 questions. Here the group uses the six words to help frame the questions. The key to the technique is in using each word twice, to explore both the problem and the 'not problem'. So the questions relate to:

- ○ What is the problem and what is not the problem?
- ○ When does it happen and when does it not happen?
- ○ Why does it happen and why does it not happen?
- ○ Where does it happen and where does it not happen?
- ○ Who contributes to causing the problem and who contributes to stopping it?

○   How do you recognize when the problem is present and how do you recognize when it is not present?

So if the problem statement was 'The high number of revised drawings circulated', the group needs to define precisely the questions that will help to explore the issue fully. Many of the questions are self-evident, for example, 'When are there a high number of revised drawings circulated?' and 'When are there not a high number of revised drawings circulated?' It is worth bearing in mind, however, that the word 'how' is usually best used to explore 'How do you recognize it when ... there are a high number of revised drawings circulated?' Also, when using the word 'why' the second time, it is best to ask 'Why were there not always a high number of revised drawings circulated?', or 'Why does the XYZ company not suffer from a high number of revised drawings circulated?' The point here is that the group should frame the questions to get the most out of them as far as their particular problem is concerned. Having defined the 12 questions, each should be written in full at the top of a sheet of flip-chart paper and posted on a wall.

Step 3

This is to review the rules of brainstorming and to post them up in the room to act as a reminder for everyone.

Step 4

This involves the group in a semi-structured brainstorming meeting aimed at eliciting both the causes and the 'not causes' of the problem. The leader should introduce this stage by stating the first question in full and asking group members to focus on it precisely. Members should then brainstorm the topic for three or four minutes and the scribe should write up the suggestions on the appropriate sheet. If during this period anyone calls out something that obviously fits under a different heading, the idea should be recorded under that heading before continuing with the original topic. This ensures that no ideas are lost. It helps, however, if everyone can concentrate attention on one question at a time.

After the group has finished the 'When' question, the leader should move on to 'When not', and the group brainstorm this topic. The next question is, 'How do you recognize when the problem is there?' and this is followed by, 'How do you recognize it when the problem isn't there?', where the group is looking at the physical manifestations of the problem.

After the 'How' section has been completed, the next questions are 'Where does the problem happen?' and 'Where doesn't the problem happen?' It is surprising how often a problem which at first seems to be pervasive in fact only affects certain places.

After the 'When', 'How' and 'Where' sections have been completed, the group can move on to 'What causes the problem?' and 'What does not cause the problem?', followed by 'Who causes it?' and 'Who does not cause it?' In brainstorming these questions the group should be careful not to blame everything on other people. Concentrating on what is our part of the problem can often yield interesting results.

This leaves the group with two more questions, 'Why is there a problem now?' and 'Why was there not a problem before?' Some problems will be the kind that seem to have been there forever. In these circumstances it may be difficult for the group to answer the last question, and if this is the case an alternative is to ask, 'Why is this problem not felt in other departments or organizations?' In completing a Six-Word Diagram, the group should not worry if there is an amount of repetition. Every suggestion should be recorded even if it has been made before and analyzed under a different heading. The strength of this technique is that it forces the group to look at the problem from all sides.

Step 5

This is to incubate the ideas on the list. As with Cause and Effect Diagrams, it is often a good idea to post the list up in the work area so that group members and others can see it. This helps to make sure that everyone knows what the group is doing, and gives the opportunity for anyone to add thoughts and ideas to the list.

Step 6

This is to analyze the completed diagram. Here the group should study the diagram and see where ideas seem to 'jump off the wall' at them, since these will be the issues to focus on in the important data collection stage that comes next. The point here is that it would be a huge task to collect data about everything relative to the problem. Equally, the Pareto principle suggests that some issues will be more important than others and so the group tries to isolate the important few issues about which to collect the facts.

In summary then, the six steps in making a Six-Word Diagram are:

1   Define the problem clearly.
2   Agree the 12 questions and write them up.
3   Review the rules of brainstorming.
4   Conduct the 12 mini-brainstorming sessions.
5   Incubate the diagram.
6   Analyze the ideas and isolate the key issues to collect data about.

SUMMARY

The analysis of problems is obviously a key step in the overall process and it is essential that the methods used help the group to get to the underlying causes rather than the symptoms of the problem. The techniques described here have been proven to be robust and powerful in a very wide range of groups involving people from all levels of the organization.

9

COLLECTING DATA

Just give me the facts, man. (US television series, *Dragnet*)

T his chapter deals with the subject of collecting information and facts. It is an area of importance in the work of problem-solving groups, as we have stressed before, because one of the distinguishing features of these groups is that they present their arguments and solutions in terms of facts rather than opinions.

Opinion-based arguments are very difficult to resolve because any one person's view can be said to be as good as the next. Discussions on such topics as 'Who is the best athlete of all time?', 'Is there a God?' and 'Which political party is right?' very rarely lead people to change their minds. In fact, more often than not, all that happens is that people end up holding even more firmly to their original opinions. The best we can hope for is probably that we end up agreeing to differ.

It is much the same in organizations up and down the land. Much conflict and frustration is a result of failures in communications caused by just this phenomenon. We all have so many opinions about so many things, and our opinions make so much sense to us, that it is often very difficult to appreciate how anyone else could fail to agree.

While some questions are difficult to collect reliable facts about, this tends not to be the case with most problems that problem-solving groups tackle. This is a great advantage since no one can argue with the facts, as long as they have been carefully collected and really do demonstrate the true situation. Arguments based on facts are not only more powerful and more likely to be accepted, they have the additional advantage of making effective communications much more possible. Problem-solving groups have demonstrated this time and time again in many different situations.

CHECK SHEETS

The main tool that problem-solving groups use for collecting data is check sheets. A check sheet is quite simply an organized way of recording information. There are many different types in common use, both at work and outside. A few examples of check sheets are shopping lists, bank statements and quality records. These are all very different types which have been specifically designed to suit the kind of information being recorded. There is usually no need for a shopping list to be any more than a list of requirements written on the back of an envelope, whereas bank statements are more formal. Quality reports are different again containing a deeper level of analysis, with the type and frequency of each defect being carefully recorded in the different sections of the report.

RULES

Check sheets can therefore come in very many different shapes and sizes, and group members need to be able to design them so that they are suitable for the particular task in hand. Before we discuss the various designs of check sheets, there are a number of rules that are common to them all. They sound obvious, but omitting them has often led to otherwise good data either having to be rejected or being very difficult to accumulate and make sense of.

RULE 1

The first of these rules is always to include the date on the document. This can be expressed as a single date, or as a week-ending or month-ending date, depending on the period covered. This does not matter too much, but it is essential to be able to tell when the data were collected if it is to mean anything. For example, to say that 6 cm of rain fell in a month is not necessarily very helpful unless we know in which month the data were collected. It could be telling us that it was a very wet July or a drier-than-average November.

RULE 2

The second convention that is common to all check sheets is to put a full title at the top of the form. This should include the location and type of information being collected. Examples might be 'computer downtime', 'Analysis of web site hits', or 'Analysis of the use of space in the stores'.

RULE 3

The third rule is that, when collecting data (a job which group members often choose to share), the form which is used should be uniform. It is very frustrating for everybody to have collected a mass of information only to find that a large-scale analysis is needed to add up the totals!

A further general observation about data collection is that there are very few fixed rules about it. It will be very much up to the group itself to decide on the best design of check sheet for the particular problem in hand. To give a reasonable basis for choice and a general grounding in check sheet design, however, we can look at three quite different types.

Number of events by type per period of time

This kind of check sheet would be used when we wish to know how often different events take place and also when they happened. So if we wanted to analyze the incoming phone calls to our section our check sheet might look like this:

ANALYSIS OF INCOMING CALLS

DATE

NAME

TIME	9-11	11-1	1-3	3-5	TOTAL
POTENTIAL CUSTOMERS					
SERVICING					
CUSTOMERS' ORDERS					
SALESMEN'S ORDERS					
CALLS FOR MANAGER					
PRIVATE CALLS					
OTHER CALLS					
TOTAL					

Type, duration and cause of event

This check sheet would be used if, for example, we had a machine that kept breaking down, say a photocopier, and we wanted to establish the patterns of its behaviour. Such a check sheet might look like this:

MACHINE BREAKDOWN ANALYSIS

MACHINE:

DATE:

TIME MACHINE DOWN	TIME FITTER ARRIVES	TIME MACHINE ON	TOTAL DOWNTIME	REASON FOR BREAKDOWN

Work flow

A different kind of check sheet would be used if we wanted to collect data about, say, the flow of work round the department. Typically this would take the form of a map of the current work stations and equipment. This would be filled in, using arrows, when there was movement of people or work round the department. Such forms can be very useful in helping to lay out the area in the most effective way.

CHOOSING CHECK SHEETS

It is up to the group to decide on which of the three types of check sheet described will be most appropriate for the problem being tackled. It is worth thinking about this carefully to make sure that the information being collected is indeed that which will help to solve the problem in hand. There is nothing more frustrating than collecting a whole load of data only to find out that it is not really relevant. It sounds rather obvious to say so, but it is surprising how many groups fall into this trap.

INFORMATION COLLECTION CRITERIA

Now we have covered the design of check sheets, it is important to discuss how much information it is necessary to collect. The main problem here is the amount of data required to give a complete picture, and group members will need to use their experience of whatever is being measured to help them make the decision. There would be no problem about this if everything happened with the same regular frequency, but of course it does not. Some things happen every now and again, in no particular pattern, others are more predictable and some are with us all the time. As far as data collection is concerned, there are very different implications for each of these situations.

There are a number of questions that problem-solving groups find it useful to ask themselves in deciding how much information to collect and when to collect it.

SEASONALITY

To what extent is the effect seasonal? If it is a seasonal effect, the data collected must take account of this. For example, we would get a very biased picture if we collected information about holidays and only collected data during the winter, or if we were investigating sickness and our information was only collected during the summer. Work examples of this might be seasonal increases and decreases in the sales of the company's products, or seasonal changes in working conditions. Where such factors have an effect, it is important for the group to take full account of them in deciding what information is needed and how much to collect.

WORKING PATTERNS

Is there anything unusual in the normal pattern of working that would affect the information collected? Most organizations are continually changing, and this can easily affect the data being collected.

OUTSIDE INFLUENCES

Is there anything unusual in the outside world that has affected, or is likely to affect, the situation? For example, a crop failure might have led to an unforeseen high level of demand for the products of some companies. Alternatively, a war in a different part of the world could affect both the demand for, and the supply of, the products of many businesses.

FREQUENCY

How often does the particular effect being considered happen in practice? Does it happen all the time, once a day, about weekly or monthly? The group needs to think about this carefully to enable it to decide on the design of the check sheet, and for how long it will be necessary to collect information.

In making these decisions the members should remember that the purpose of collecting the facts is to develop a full picture of the situation, not just a small part of it. It will not help members devising an effective solution if the group only collects information for a day when it really takes a month for the complete picture to emerge.

Problem-solving groups are effective for many reasons, not least of which is that they present their arguments in terms of facts rather than opinions. Check sheets are the main mechanism used for data collection and group members are in the best position to draw them up, since there are many different possible designs. The guidelines for doing this have been covered in this chapter. In summary, the key points to remember are:

O   Always enter the date and the full heading on each check sheet.
O   Make sure that each person collecting data has the same design of check sheet.
O   Make sure that the data collected are really those which are needed to help solve the problem.
O   Think about what other factors, inside the company or in the outside world, are influencing the data being collected.
O   Make sure that sufficient data are collected to show the full picture, not just part of it.

SUMMARY

If there is one thing that will give a group a better than average chance of having its recommendations accepted, it is if they are based on facts rather than opinions.

10

INTERPRETING DATA

There are lies, damned lies and statistics. (Benjamin Disraeli)

This chapter deals with the question of how to interpret data and get the best out of it for the purpose of solving the problem. Unfortunately, very many people have a prejudice against numbers and freeze at the very mention of the word statistics! In fact, many managers use statistics in the same way that a drunk uses a lamp-post – more for support than illumination!

With this in mind, and considering that problem-solving groups need to do their work on the basis of facts, not opinions, there is a need for some organized tools for looking at data and exploring it to reap the most benefit from it.

PARETO CHARTS

A number of tools have proved to be invaluable in helping groups understand the facts they have collected, the first of which is the Pareto Chart. Vilfredo Pareto was an Italian economist who researched the distribution of wealth in his country. He found that 80 per cent of the wealth was in the hands of 20 per cent of the people. It soon became clear that this was a general rule that applied to many things and the so-called 80:20 law was born and Pareto's place in history assured. The Pareto Chart is a way of showing data graphically to see if a few of the causes really are contributing to much of the effect.

There are five steps in the construction of a Pareto diagram and it may facilitate understanding to work through a simple example. The case in point comes from a small printing company which was trying to establish what were the big problems to tackle.

STEP 1

Organize the data that have been collected in descending order of priority as shown in this figure and add up the total.

Problem	No. of occasions
Printing defects	38
Overruns	13
Stripping errors	12
Packing damage	7
Wrong paper	4
Ink problems	3
Damage in transit	3
Falling off conveyor	2
Sticky paper	2
Platen balance	1
Total	**85**

STEP 2

Distinguish from this list where the cut-off point should come between the vital few and the trivial many. With Pareto Charts the miscellaneous are usually grouped together under the heading 'Other'. Having done this, the cumulative column is filled in to give a running total.

Problem	No. of occasions		Cumulative
Printing defects	38		38
Overruns	13		51
Stripping errors	12		63
Packing damage	7		70
Wrong paper	4		
Ink problems	3		
Damage in transit	3	'Other' = 15	85
Falling off conveyor	2		
Sticky paper	2		
Platen balance	1		
Total	**85**		

STEP 3

Prepare the graph. The vertical column is always for the variable data, the number of occasions, the cost and so on; the horizontal axis is for the categories themselves. The vertical scale should go up as far as the total of the data collected, in this case 85 problems. As far as the horizontal scale is concerned, it should be divided up into as many categories as there are, remembering that 'Other' counts as one, so in this instance there are four main categories, plus one for 'Other' making five.

An unusual feature of the Pareto Chart comes next with another vertical axis but this time on the right-hand side. The purpose of this is to make it easy to interpret the chart in percentage figures. This only needs to be a rough-and-ready figure so there is no real need to calculate the percentages mathematically. Obviously 100 per cent equals the total number from the left-hand vertical column (85), half of this is 50 per cent and so on.

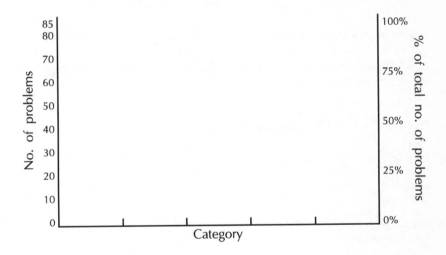

STEP 4

Enter the data from the chart onto the graph. This is done first by entering the items in bar chart form, always leaving the 'Other' column until last. Having done this, the cumulative line should be entered in the way illustrated.

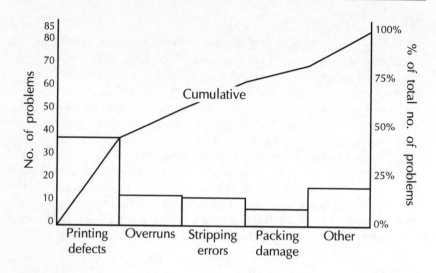

As can be seen from the completed diagram, the top three problems (30 per cent of the original 10 categories) account for about 75 per cent of the problems experienced. The Pareto Chart, because of its format, highlights these key areas and helps groups to establish priorities for attention and action.

Problem	No. of occasions	Cost (£)
Overruns	13	6630
Printing defects	38	2140
Packing damage	7	1050
Stripping errors	12	590
Damage in transit	3	340
Sticky paper	2	190
Wrong paper	4	108
Ink problems	3	58
Platen balance	1	54
Falling off conveyor	2	10

At this point it is important to note that problem-solving groups need to explore thoroughly the data they collect rather than simply to take the most obvious conclusion as being valid. These data are a case in point. It would have been easy for the group to have concluded that the key problem to tackle was 'Printing defects', but fortunately they decided, as Step 5, to explore the data further by finding out the costs associated with each of the problems and to construct another Pareto Chart using this information.

Problem	No. of occasions	Cost (£)		Cumulative (£)
Overruns	13	6630		6630
Printing defects	38	2140		8770
Packing damage	7	1050		9820
Stripping errors	12	590		10410
Damage in transit	3	340		10750
Sticky paper	2	190		
Wrong paper	4	108		
Ink problems	3	58	'Other' = 420	11170
Platen balance	1	54		
Falling off conveyor	2	10		
Total	**85**	**11170**		

When the group had obtained the cost figures, members then reorganized the data into a new descending order of priority based on cost rather than number of problems. The results were startlingly different as shown in the above table. The 'Other' column and the cumulative figures were then added together.

This second Pareto Chart vividly demonstrated the priority as far as cost was concerned.

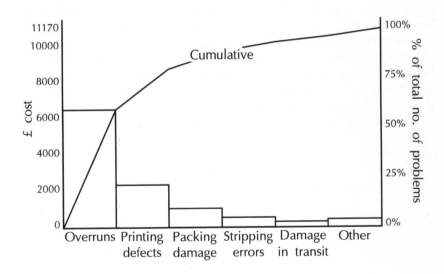

Here the top two cost items (20 per cent of the original ten) account for about 80 per cent of the total cost of all the problems, and the main item, overruns, by itself causes about 60 per cent of the cost.

The important lesson here is to reinforce the point that data are there to be explored thoroughly. The Pareto Chart is a simple and vivid way of doing this and has a place in any problem-solving tool kit.

The five steps in constructing a Pareto diagram are:

1   Organize the data in descending order of priority and total it.
2   Establish the cut-off point for the 'Other' category and add the cumulative column.
3   Prepare the graph adding in the percentage column on the right.
4   Complete the chart with bars and the cumulative line.
5   Explore other possible Pareto Charts using the same data.

HISTOGRAMS

A second tool for helping to interpret data is the histogram, which is a different kind of bar chart from the Pareto diagram. Here we are looking at one issue or problem and trying to make sense of the data we have collected. The data could relate to how tall people are, how much they weigh or the size of their feet. Equally, it could be about the car fuel consumption, how long vehicles go between breakdowns and a million and one other things. The point here is that most sets of data fall into a so-called Normal Distribution, that is, there will be a lot of medium height people and fewer short or tall ones in most populations. Equally, many cars will do about 50 to 70 kilometres per litre (kpl) of fuel whereas relatively few will do 15 kpl or 150 kpl. A histogram helps pick up these patterns and expresses them in a graphical form which can help groups to highlight whether a piece of data is in the mainstream, or at an extreme. It measures frequency.

There are four steps in constructing a histogram.

STEP 1

Take the data that have been collected and establish the highest and lowest values. The mass of data shown overleaf represents the time it took to answer the telephone on the switchboard of a particular insurance company.

Time taken to answer telephone (seconds)   **w/e xx/xx/200x**

26.5	22	20	26	28
34	24	27	20	29
18	27	26	26	25.5
34	26	28.5	20.5	23
22	25.5	22	33	27
25.5	27	31	28	30.5
21	26.5	22	23.5	33.5
37	27.5	22.5	29	28
30	18	24	24	25
16	24	30	26	32.5

Longest time = 37 seconds
Shortest time = 16 seconds
Range = 22 seconds

The data were collected by the members of a problem-solving group tackling a problem related to customer service. The supervisor of the switchboard area was a member of the group and suggested this information be collected over the period of a week.

STEP 2

Divide the range up into a number of equal-sized slots. There is no fixed rule about the number of slots but it should normally be somewhere between 8 and 12. In this case the group decided on slots of 2 seconds. Then each of the entries is logged against one or other slot.

Time taken to answer telephone (seconds)   **w/e xx/xx/200x**

16 – 17.9	|		= 1
18 – 19.9	| |		= 2
20 – 21.9	| | | |		= 4
22 – 23.9	++++	| |	= 7
24 – 25.9	++++	| | |	= 8
26 – 27.9	++++ ++++	| |	= 12
28 – 29.9	++++	|	= 6
30 – 31.9	| | | |		= 4
32 – 33.9	| | |		= 3
34 – 35.9	| |		= 2
36 – 37.9	|		= 1

STEP 3

Prepare the graph with the vertical column for the number of occasions and the horizontal axis for the seconds delay. In this case, the time delay was divided up into ten equal sections from the minimum to the maximum, making up the horizontal axis, and the highest number of entries for one slot was 12 which is the highest that is needed for the vertical axis.

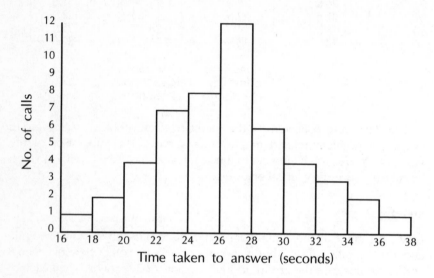

As can be seen from this histogram, the original mass of apparently meaningless data does actually fall into a very recognizable normal distribution. Given this, the group was better able to define what the service standard should be, to analyze the causes of the delays and to improve the performance of the switchboard significantly, until it could claim to be answering 95 per cent of calls within 10 seconds. The switchboard itself was a major contributor to this progress and, amongst other things, took on board the responsibility for keeping track of its own performance on an ongoing basis.

Of course, not all data fall conveniently into a Normal Distribution. Other main possibilities are as follows.

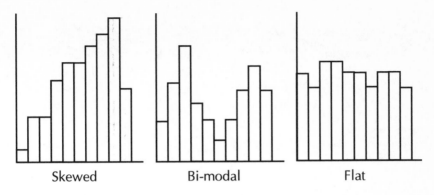

Skewed   Bi-modal   Flat

STEP 4

As with all data, the question the group should be asking, and the fourth step, is 'Why this distribution and what is it telling us that we can use in helping to solve the problem at hand?'

The four steps in constructing a histogram are therefore:

1   List the data and establish the highest and lowest points and the range from top to bottom.
2   Divide the range into a number of equal-sized slots and allocate each piece of data to one or other slot.
3   Construct the histogram.
4   Ask, 'Why this distribution, what is it telling us?'

SUMMARY

Pareto Charts and histograms are two tools that are very often applicable for helping to interpret the data collected by problem-solving groups. There will be other occasions when simple line graphs will suffice, or pie charts or a range of other ways of visualizing the figures. Putting the information into visual forms often aids understanding of the data and thereby assists the problem-solving process, so groups will be well advised to use these tools wherever possible.

11

FINDING SOLUTIONS

When you have eliminated the impossible, whatever remains, however improbable, must be the truth. (Sir Arthur Conan Doyle)

Not only do problem-solving groups need tools and techniques to identify and analyze problems and opportunities, they also require them for finding solutions. A spread of techniques encouraging both analytical and creative thought is needed here since different groups, and indeed different problems, will require different approaches.

The techniques summarized in this chapter cover a wide range of possibilities and will be useful additions to the 'kit bag' of tools held by individuals and groups. They are not all interchangeable; indeed, some of them are only designed to be used in specific circumstances, either to do with the nature of the group or the nature of the problem being tackled.

TECHNIQUE 1: SOLUTIONS FISHBONE DIAGRAM

The Solutions Fishbone Diagram is a useful technique in a wide range of situations. It can be used analytically but is often best treated as a creative technique. It has the added advantage that the members of the groups are already likely to be familiar with the Cause and Effect Diagram. This is useful since the Solutions Fishbone Diagram is simply a different version of it, but rather than being used to analyze causes, it is used to find possible solutions. Using this technique involves six stages.

STEP 1

Write the problem statement in a box on the left-hand side of three sheets of flip-chart paper that have been posted up side by side on a wall.

STEP 2

Agree within the group the main categories which will be relevant with their current problem. The basic headings which are used for both the Cause and Effect Diagram and the Solutions Fishbone Diagram are:

○   People
○   Environment
○   Method
○   Plant
○   Equipment
○   Materials.

The group should remember that other broad categories may be included and that basic categories can be excluded if appropriate. It is important, however, to remember that these main ribs of the fish relate to broad categories of idea and not to the detailed suggestions themselves, which forms the body of the analysis.

STEP 3

Draw in the main ribs of the fishbone and label the ribs with the agreed categories as shown in the diagram.

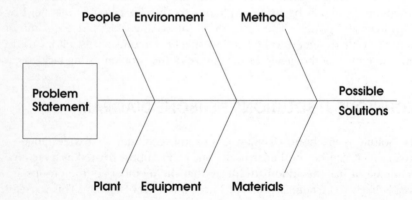

STEP 4

The leader should review the rules of brainstorming, again reinforce them and then post them up prior to running the brainstorming meeting to generate possible solutions. Remember to group ideas which are linked by using 'sub-ribs' and 'sub-sub-ribs' as in the illustration.

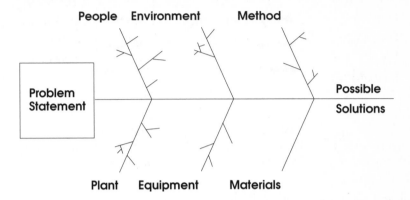

STEP 5

Incubate the diagram for long enough to let the ideas sink in.

STEP 6

Evaluate the ideas and highlight what the group considers to be the 'Pareto' items.

The six steps in using the Solutions Fishbone thus are:

1   Write up the problem statement.
2   Agree the main ribs.
3   Draw up the diagram.
4   Brainstorm solution possibilities.
5   Incubate.
6   Evaluate diagram for best solution ideas.

TECHNIQUE 2: FORCE-FIELD ANALYSIS

Force-Field Analysis was developed by Kurt Lewin to help people visualize problems. It is a method which mainly uses analytical thinking. It can be applied in a wide range of situations and should be a part of the tool kit of all problem-solving groups. Force-Field Analysis tells us that a problem is made up of a balance of two opposing sets of forces. One set is trying to push the current situation and make it better; these are the driving forces. The opposing forces are trying to push the current situation and make it worse; these are the restraining forces. We can show this diagrammatically as follows.

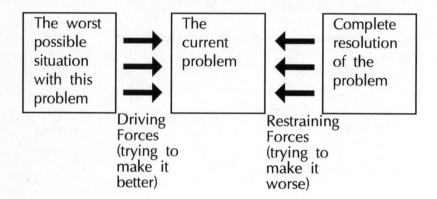

There are six steps involved in using Force-Field Analysis to generate possible solutions:

STEP 1

This is to get the group to define the worst possible situation relative to the problem, and also to state the ideal situation. The current state of play should already be clear, having analyzed the problem, collected data about it and interpreted these data. Write up the best and worst scenarios on separate pieces of flip-chart paper and post them with three blank sheets of, preferably lined, flip-chart paper between them as shown below.

The Worst Possible Situation		IMP	INF		IMP	INF		The Ideal Situation
			US	OTH		US	OTH	
Driving Forces								Restraining Forces
➡								⬅
➡								⬅
Flipchart 1		Flipchart 2						Flipchart 3

Key: IMP = Importance of the forces
      INF = How much can the forces be influenced by ...
      US   = The group
      OTH = Others outside the group

STEP 2

Discuss and agree the restraining forces that are stopping the group from moving towards the ideal, and are pushing towards the worst situation. List them on the flip-chart paper. Once all the forces have been identified, get the group to rank these forces for importance, using the scale shown below.

Definition	Rating
A key influence – vital to shift this force if the problem is to be solved	4
An important influence – will definitely help if we can change this force	3
Useful progress could be made by changing the force, but not likely to be of great importance overall	2
Little influence on the problem	1

These ratings should be recorded in the appropriate column, as shown in the diagram above.

STEP 3

Repeat the procedure outlined in Step 2, but this time focus on the driving forces.

STEP 4

Get the group to look at the two sets of forces and discuss how easily the forces can be influenced. Again a rating system should be used and the one shown below works well.

Definition	Rating
A force that is easily changed	4
A force that would change with effort	3
A difficult force to change entirely, but possible with much effort to change it a little	2
A fixed unchanging force	1

In rating the forces in this way the group should consider who can exert influence over them. The same ranking system should be used to fill in the columns marked 'Us', which measures the ability of the group to influence the force, and also the 'Others' column which looks at how easily other people can exert influence. Both columns should be completed for all the forces before proceeding to the next stage.

STEP 5

At this stage, the group is ready to assess which forces it should focus its attention on. This can be done numerically by adding up the 'scores' for importance and ability to influence (either 'Us' or 'Others'). When this has been done, the group needs to look for high scores since these indicate that something is both important and easy to influence, either directly by the group or by others. Once the group has highlighted where it should focus, it can begin to develop its action plan, which is Step 6.

STEP 6

As an aid to effective action planning, the group should answer a number of questions, which will help identify the specific action steps aimed at reducing/eliminating the restraining forces and increasing the driving forces. It is generally better to begin by constructing action plans to reduce or eliminate the restraining forces, since this is the most powerful way of solving the problem.

The questions which will help ensure effective action planning are:

O   What exactly needs to be done?
O   Who will do what?
O   When will it be done?
O   How will it be augmented and supported?

Force-Field Analysis is a very powerful tool for generating solution ideas and then prioritizing them, and what is more problem-solving group members tend to enjoy using it when they have mastered the steps.

The steps in using the Force-Field Analysis technique are therefore:

1   Define the worst and best possible situations.
2   Identify and rank restraining forces.
3   Identify and rank driving forces.
4   Assess the possibility of influencing the forces.
5   Highlight priority areas.
6   Action plan to solve problem.

TECHNIQUE 3: THE DELPHI

The Delphi technique is useful in a wide range of situations, and especially in a group where there are silent members or others who do not either take or get the chance to have their full say. There are all too many groups like this, and the quality of their solutions is often affected by the fact that only some members of the group have contributed their ideas. This situation will also very often have an influence on the commitment of members, especially silent ones, to the solution.

There are five steps involved in using the Delphi approach. The group will have analyzed the problem and collected data about it by the time this technique is used.

STEP 1

This is for the leader of the group, or facilitator if appropriate, to review the problem, the analysis and the data collected. Where possible, the relevant flip charts should be posted to act as a reminder for members.

STEP 2

This involves giving members 20 x 13 cm cards and asking them to list possible solutions, one per card. Members should be encouraged to think creatively and to generate more than one possibility. At this stage they should work alone. This stage can be organized as part of a meeting, or members can be asked to complete the task between meetings.

STEP 3

The leader collects all the cards and combines the ideas into a list. Repetitive items should be combined but no indication should be given that any idea was suggested by more than one person. This activity can be done during the meeting by collecting cards as they are completed, though it does take some time and might leave the members with nothing to do for a while. Alternatively, it can be accomplished between meetings.

Once the list has been completed and written up on the flip chart, it should be read aloud by the leader.

STEP 4

Members should be asked individually to rank the importance of the solution ideas and to write down their ranking on a 20 x 13 cm card, with 1 being the highest priority and most important solution if the problem is to be solved. When this has been done, the cards should be collected and the results recorded on a flip chart in the following format.

Solution Idea	Member							
	1	2	3	4	5	6	7	8
1								
2								
3								
4								

STEP 5

With the views of all group members having been recorded, generate a discussion with the aim of agreeing which solution ideas the team should focus on. At this stage it is essential that minority views are both heard and respected. The leader and facilitator must be very sensitive to this, since it is all too easy for the voice of dissenters to be lost. This technique ensures that all views are recorded, and it is vital now that they are heard and properly considered. The five steps in using the Delphi are as follows:

1   Review the problem analysis and data.
2   Generate solution ideas individually.
3   Combine ideas onto one list.

4   Individual ranking and recording of solution ideas.
5   Discuss rankings and agree solutions by consensus.

TECHNIQUE 4: SWAPPING

Swapping is designed specifically for situations where the group has polarized into two camps, each of which is clinging firmly to its own solution. This situation happens quite frequently and can lead to the breakdown of communication in the group, and ultimately to the group collapsing. The swapping technique tries to encourage the rival factions to listen to each other, by getting them to present the opposition's case. There are five steps to this approach.

STEP 1

Brief group members. Here an outline of the method is presented to the group and the objective is described as being to try to break the deadlock that exists as far as the solution to the problem is concerned, and to come up with the best possible solution for this group as a whole. It should be stressed that it is important for the group to resolve this issue and that this is a serious attempt to do so.

STEP 2

Divide the group into the two opposing camps and instruct each to develop a presentation of the opposing view which it will deliver to the other group. The presentation should not only represent the other case fairly and accurately, but the groups should be instructed to include at least two additional supporting ideas.

The preparation of the presentations should be done during group meetings, and relevant information relating to the case should be made freely available. The facilitator and leader need to play an active role in this preparation stage in ensuring that the two groups are taking the exercise seriously and that they have access to the information they need.

STEP 3

Get the sub-groups to present. The presentations themselves should be made in a formal manner with the facilitator being assigned as a referee to ensure fair play. The presentations should, where possible, involve posting the main points on flip chart paper round the room. After each presentation, questions may be asked for clarification of meaning, but no evaluation should be made. The leader and facilitator should take any reasonable steps to make the atmosphere one of serious, but enjoyable, endeavour.

STEP 4

Once both the presentations have been made they are critiqued by the opposing camp, and the main points of the critique should be recorded on the flip chart. The facilitator should introduce this fourth stage by insisting on a 'describe, don't judge' rule. In other words, people should describe their feelings, views and reactions, not judge the intent of the opposition.

STEP 5

Once the critiques have been completed and the main points recorded, they should be posted round the room along with the charts summarizing the two presentations. At this final stage, the facilitator and leader should engage the group in a discussion aimed at achieving a new consensus of all group members which, it should be stressed, will be better than both the original solutions because it has additional features, and furthermore because it has the support of all members. Indeed, an entirely new solution might emerge at this stage, though it is essential to avoid any easy compromises that simply avoid the issue and do not really solve the problem.

This technique will require a high degree of facilitative and leadership skill, since it will only be used when an impasse has been reached. Having said this, with careful planning around this basic structure, and with sensitive handling of the meetings themselves, it can be an immensely powerful way of increasing understanding of the other view, re-creating team spirit, achieving an even better solution than either of the originals and putting the group back on track with a solution with which all members can agree.

The swapping technique thus involves five stages, as follows:

1   Brief team members.
2   Prepare presentations of opposing view.
3   Present.
4   Critique presentations.
5   Agree new solutions through consensus.

TECHNIQUE 5: COLLAGES AND FANTASIES

Occasionally, groups get into a situation where they want to tackle a problem that is abstract and non-tangible. Sometimes such problems and the groups' views about them are very difficult to put into words. This clearly makes it hard to describe and discuss them both within the group and with others outside, including management. It is in this situation that the technique of collages and fantasies can be of help, since it communicates first of all through the visual sense. Once the visual message has been created, it is often much easier to verbalize it as well.

This technique will probably have a limited application, but is useful for the group to know about. If groups do get into the situations outlined above, it is very difficult for them to get out of them without such a technique as this. It involves six steps.

STEP 1

Preparation: the facilitator or leader should prepare for the meeting by gathering together a range of magazines and newspapers. These should be selected at random and need to include different types of publication. It is important not to end up with a selection of pure business publications. Include, amongst others, sporting, household and travel magazines, serious and popular newspapers – the wider the range the better. Do take some risks since all kinds of magazines can assist this process. At this stage, scissors, glue and tape will also be needed.

STEP 2

Describe the technique to the group as one which will help to visualize the present and desired situation. The group may need reminding of the difficulty it has had in describing the situation in words and may need encouragement to use an additional method for communicating, visual plus verbal, as opposed to purely verbal. The technique involves asking the group to create two collages/fantasies, one describing the present situation, and the second the ideal towards which the group is aiming. A collage is simply a composition of bits and pieces stuck together on a background. The bits and pieces can be cuttings from the magazines and newspapers or anything else that the group has ready access to (except perhaps for bits and pieces of people!). The background will usually be flip-chart paper, though this need not be the case.

STEP 3

Since this is likely to be a new and unusual exercise for many of the members, it is important to set the scene carefully. The group is being asked to create a visual interpretation of how it sees things currently relating to the issue, and also its vision or fantasy of the future. The group will need to use its creative talent to express these views. A non-critical, fun, creative atmosphere is vital here, and needs to be engendered by the facilitator and leader.

STEP 4

This involves the group, including the leader and if appropriate the facilitator, creating the two collages. This will usually be best organized as separate activities one after the other, though on occasions it could be beneficial to work on both simultaneously.

The area where the work is to be accomplished needs to be suitably open, to enable members to walk around and be freely creative. Often the collages are created on the floor, and people spend their time sitting down, walking around, cutting out words and pictures, talking in sub-groups, holding mini-group meetings. It often gives the impression of chaos, but it is important to allow this to happen, indeed to encourage it, since out of this often comes a crystal-clear view of what is, and what needs to be.

The time allowed for the creation of the collages will vary. In many circumstances it will be appropriate to allow a meeting for each. Sometimes more than this will be required and at other times groups may wish to try and accomplish both statements in one meeting, though this would be rushing things.

STEP 5

Having completed the collages, the fifth step is to develop a verbal presentation of what they represent and mean. This should be done through group discussion, and at this stage alterations and additions can be made to the product.

STEP 6

In the final step, the group needs to use its output. This can take two main forms. First, if the group has used the technique to try and 'unstick' itself it may now be able to continue with addressing the issue in the conventional way. Alternatively, it may be that the group needs to present its collages to senior management or other interested and affected parties. In this case, it is important for the group or facilitator to explain the technique, and the background as far as this problem is concerned, before the collages are revealed.

'Collages and fantasies' is a very powerful technique which uses the visual sense to assist normal verbal presentation. Though not appropriate in every situation, it has a surprisingly wide range of uses once it is understood and confidence is gained in its use.

The six steps in using the collages and fantasies technique are:

1   Prepare by gathering magazines, papers, tape, glue and scissors.
2   Describe the technique to the group.
3   Set the scene for using the technique in relation to the current problem.
4   Create the collages.
5   Develop verbal presentations.
6   Use the output.

It is useful for problem-solving groups to have a variety of tools available for generating solution possibilities, and different methods will be appropriate in different circumstances. Whichever method is used, however, it will be necessary for the group to subject its preferred solution to a rigorous cost-benefit analysis, since solutions are not likely to be welcomed if the costs exceed the benefits.

COSTS AND BENEFITS

A person selling raffle tickets for £1 each when the first prize is worth 50p, would be unlikely to persuade many people to buy. So it is with management decision-making. A proposal which would cost £100,000 to implement and would yield a once-off benefit of £50,000 would be unlikely to be accepted, unless there were other hidden benefits associated with it.

Many solutions recommended by groups, of course, yield benefits that carry on year after year, but only cost money at the start, and in these situations the group needs to be able to calculate the payback period for its solution. Different companies have different thoughts about the payback period they work to. Sometimes a six- or seven-year payback period is acceptable, but in general it is more likely to be two or three years. In any case, the shorter the payback period, the more chance the group has of selling its solution.

Some solutions, however, are very difficult if not impossible to evaluate in this way. For example, improvements in working conditions, or a better organized filing system are very difficult to quantify in monetary terms. In situations such as these, there should be no problem if the solution costs nothing, but if it does involve some outlay it will be important to establish what other benefits will come out of the solution.

The point here is that the cost–benefit relation does not have to be expressed in terms of money: it could be time saved, relationships between people getting better, communications between departments improving and many other kinds of benefit. Trying to see things from top management's point of view in this way will repay the group many times over and help mutual understanding.

SUMMARY

It is obvious that no problem is solved before it is solved! Different circumstances will require different techniques to find the correct solution – some will need an analytical approach, others will be more amenable to creative solutions, which is why group problem-solvers need to have a variety of tools at their disposal.

12

COST-BENEFIT ANALYSIS

You pays your money and you takes your choice. (Punch)

A theme that has been stressed throughout this book is that if we wish to solve problems successfully and to have our recommendations accepted, then we must base our work on facts rather than opinions. Most people will accept this in theory but many of us lapse back into opinion-based problem-solving very quickly unless we are forced into the discipline at all stages of the process. Earlier chapters have covered the collection and interpretation of data as a prerequisite to the analysis of any problem, and Chapter 11 dealt with the subject of finding solutions. This is often thought of as being the last step, but in fact it is not, especially if we are interested in having our solutions accepted, and even more importantly, implemented and monitored. The acceptance of the solution proposed by a problem-solving group depends in part on the analysis and the solution, but ultimately it depends on an assessment of what will be achieved by the solution and the investment of resources that will be required to achieve the results. In other words, the decision will rest on a cost-benefit analysis, and this is the subject of this chapter.

DEFINITION

Cost-benefit analysis, as the phrase suggests, involves an analysis and comparison of the costs which will be incurred in pursuing a course of action and the benefits that will be achieved as a result. The term may sound technical and complex, but in fact we undertake cost-benefit analyzes routinely in the normal course of our lives; it is just that we do not call it by that name. When we decide to build an extension onto the back of our house we find out how much it would cost, and then we justify that cost in terms of the benefits that the extension would provide. We do this both in terms of our own comfort and convenience and also the assumed increase in the value of the property as a result of this investment. If the equation does not work out or does not feel right we do not proceed; if it does, we do. This is an example of a cost-benefit analysis. Every time we ask ourselves, 'Is it worth it?' we are asking a question about the balance between costs and benefits. Overall then, though the term might sound technical, cost-benefit analysis, like so much of the problem-solving process, is no more than organized common sense.

Within the problem-solving process, this element forms the next step after the group has come to an initial view about its preferred solution. This will have been done using the data that will have been collected, and having explored all possible solutions, but until the costs and benefits of the solution have been calculated the group is not in a position to make its final recommendation, so this step is an essential one and it is vitally important that the group retains an open mind and does not get too committed to its preferred course of action until this stage has been completed.

COST-BENEFIT ANALYSIS STEPS

STEP 1

Cost-benefit analysis involves four steps. The first is to use the group to make an assessment of the costs that will be involved in implementing the proposed solution. Some of these costs will be simple to identify but there are often others that are not so obvious but may well be significant. Because of this there is a good case for thinking creatively at this point. The technique that should be used to facilitate this is brainstorming. This technique was described in detail in Chapter 6 and it is essential to use the method properly. All too often so-called brainstorming sessions merely involve a straightforward listing of obvious possibilities, because they are not set up and run correctly. The range of possible costs for any solution can be very wide and it is important that all the relevant ones are captured. Certainly the costs will not be limited to the straightforward investment which may be required in new equipment, components, software and so on. Other categories which could be relevant include such items as time lost, both human and machine downtime whilst the solution was being implemented, lost output, installation costs, overtime, training, briefing, morale, and many more. Wherever possible, the costs that are identified should be converted into monetary terms. This is because money is the universal language of business and is easy to understand. However, note that not all costs can be easily expressed in this way. There will be occasions, not only when the significant costs are not easily quantified, but also when the decision is swayed by non-quantifiable costs and benefits which, for a variety of reasons, could be viewed as being more important in the overall scheme of things.

STEP 2

The second step in constructing a cost-benefit analysis is to go through a similar process focusing this time on the benefits that can be expected from the solution. Again some of the benefits may well be fairly self-evident, but it is quite likely that there will be others that are not and the group will want to tease these out so that they can judge the whole case. Again the technique of brainstorming should be used, making sure that the rules are adhered to carefully. In calculating the benefits wherever possible use the language of money, but it is essential when doing this that credibility is not stretched too far since this could undermine the whole of the case that is being proposed. The group is unlikely to achieve credibility if it bases its recommendation on a tenuous judgement that the solution would improve communication in the company by 2.5 per cent and that this was worth £105,755.86 per annum!

Not every factor can, or indeed should, be converted to money; sometimes it is necessary to use different cost-benefit ratios. For example, the advantages of a particular solution might include improved working conditions, employee morale, better relationships between individuals or departments or enhancement of the culture of the organization. Benefits such as these all have a value, especially to forward-thinking managements, and groups should always include them in their argument where relevant.

Another factor that groups come up against in calculating the anticipated benefits of their solution is that it is sometimes difficult to be precise, and so the group needs to know how to handle this eventuality. The key here is to understand that it is perfectly alright to use estimates as long as the logic of the calculation is made clear. It will also usually make sense for the group to be conservative in its estimate rather than over optimistic. All too often groups which are over optimistic in their predictions will be questioned and will end up having to change their figures to the detriment of their case. On the other hand, the group that is prudent in its estimate can turn this into an advantage when selling its solution benefit by stating that 'even on a conservative basis the benefits amount to …'. This is powerful because it shows that the group is behaving responsibly, and still producing solutions that will benefit the organization.

STEP 3

The third step in constructing a cost-benefit analysis is to lay out the outputs of Steps 1 and 2 and to get the group to subject the analysis to a number of questions, the first of which is, 'If this was your money you were talking of spending, what would you do?' To answer this question usefully it is necessary for group members to be honest with themselves and each other. There is nothing wrong with coming to the conclusion that the benefits are not sufficient, or that the cost is too high, since the group can always go back and explore other possible solutions. It is much better to recognize this situation, if it exists, and to deal with it, rather than to risk the weakness of the solution being exposed, or worse, a solution being implemented that the group knows is not a good use of the organization's resources.

If the group can genuinely say that it believes in the investment there are a number of other questions that must be asked before the final decision is made, and these relate to the guidelines which are likely to be used by the organization in assessing the proposed investment. The first of these concerns the payback period. This is the length of time that will be necessary for the benefits of the solution to pay for the cost of implementation. Thus, if the costs of a solution were £10,000 and the benefits were £5,000 per annum, the payback period would be two years. Obviously, the shorter the payback period the more attractive will be the solution as far as the organization is concerned. There are some guidelines but they do vary from organization to organization and are also affected by what is being purchased. For example, a new personal computer might have to pay for itself within a year, whereas a new computer system could be allowed three or four years to pay for itself. The group members must understand the conventions used in their company, and someone should be given the task of finding out by asking the finance director or another senior manager as appropriate.

In a similar vein, there are other factors that will influence the reaction of the organization to the group's proposal and which should be taken into account. The main ones are the state the company is in and the amount of the investment being recommended. It would do no good recommending an excellent solution to a problem that would cost more than the organization could afford to pay, indeed, this would only lead to frustration on everyone's part. Furthermore, groups at this stage of the problem-solving process should remember that an organization's resources are limited and that there is always competition for them. Solutions that do not involve major investment will always be the most attractive. The group should go out of its way to attempt to minimize the financial investment required to implement the proposed solution.

STEP 4

If the proposed solution stands up to this scrutiny, the group is ready to begin preparing its case, and will, of course, want to present it in as positive a way as possible. This is the final step in the cost-benefit analysis. Chapter 13 on presenting solutions deals with many of the methods groups use to make presentations, but before we tackle this, the group should consider how best to put forward the figures which will be central to its case. Clearly the greater the benefit and lower the cost, the easier this will be, but any financial benefits should be calculated on an annual basis since to say that the solution will yield a benefit of £10,000 a year sounds more interesting and substantial than to say £200 a week. Other benefits should be looked at in the same light and the question asked as to how best to present them for full impact.

SUMMARY

This part of the problem-solving process is essential for success. It is no good developing a wonderful solution that is then rejected because the group has not done its homework as far as thinking through the implications for the organization. Once this step has been completed the group is ready to pull its work together in a presentation where it will sell the benefits of its work, and this is the subject of the next chapter.

PART III
FOLLOWING THROUGH

❖

13

PRESENTING SOLUTIONS

How to win friends and influence people. (Dale Carnegie)

Problem-solving groups have the responsibility for selling their solutions to the appropriate decision-makers. The normal mechanism for doing this is that the group gives a presentation of its recommendations. This chapter concentrates on this subject and examines ways of ensuring that the presentation goes well. Problem-solving groups are concerned with getting things done, and since the decision about the implementation of the group's recommendations will generally rest with senior management, it is essential that the group members know how to make their presentation effective.

There is little doubt that presentations are a very powerful mechanism for achieving action, which is why they are so important. Presentations are rather like the tip of an iceberg; they are the visible part of the work, but they depend for success on all the other activities that have gone on beneath the surface – the problem identification, analysis, data collection and so on. A presentation can only be as good as the quality of these other functions, and if a group has done its work well, it will show through in the presentations it gives.

REASONS FOR PRESENTATIONS

First, it will be useful to consider why presentations are the mechanism

105

favoured by problem-solving groups for selling their solutions; why not write a memo, for example, or have a meeting with the single person who can make the decision? There are four main reasons for presentations usually being the most appropriate method:

1   Although one person may be authorized to make the decision, there are often other people who will be affected and, as such, need to be kept informed.

2   By inviting everyone who will be affected to come to the presentation, it is possible for them to influence the decision, and this will help to build their commitment to it.

3   Presentations give a topic the importance it deserves by focusing attention on it. This helps to ensure that the problem and its solution are looked at from all angles by those concerned.

4   Presentations give group members the chance to sell their work, and the improvement process generally. More people have been converted to a belief in the value of group problem-solving activities as a mechanism for improvement as a result of attending presentations than for any other reason.

STAGES IN PRESENTATION

There are three broad stages which we need to consider:

○   preparation for the meeting
○   the meeting itself
○   follow-up after the meeting.

PREPARATION

It is often said that half of persuasion is preparation, and this seems to be borne out in practice. There are six aspects of preparation which need to be considered.

OBJECTIVES

At the outset the group needs to be clear about what it is trying to get out of the presentation. In some circumstances the group may be aiming for a clear decision at the end of the meeting. On other occasions possibly a commitment to further investigation is what is being sought. There are many possible goals and it is important that members do not lose sight of what they are trying to achieve, since this will influence the type of presentation they make and the points they cover during it. For example, a meeting to review progress being made by a group that is working on a particularly long and complicated problem will be different from a presentation of a relatively small solution where the group is looking for an immediate decision.

POINT OF VIEW

Having thought through what it is the group is trying to achieve, members can move on to the second aspect of preparation, which is to try to understand the way of thinking of those who will be attending, and to see matters from their point of view. One of the main preoccupations of managers attending any presentations is that time and money are scarce resources and that it is simply not possible to do everything that one might like to do. In deciding whether or not to allocate time and money to different projects, the good manager will be balancing the costs and benefits. The cost-benefit equation is an important part of management decision-making, as we have learned, and problem-solving groups need to be able to think in the same terms, since people are unlikely to agree to do something if the costs are greater than the benefits. Thus the members of the group need to think through the questions posed in Chapter 12 and also consider any knowledge that they have about the individuals who will be deciding the fate of their recommendation. Some people are only likely to listen to proposals that generate tangible financial benefits, whereas others will also be interested in other non-quantifiable gains. Trying to see matters from the listeners' point of view in this way will repay the group many times over and help mutual understanding.

LOGIC AND LENGTH

It is important to be sure that the presentation is logical and of the right length. The normal sequence should be to:

O outline the problem that the group has tackled
O go through the initial analysis
O explain the reasoning behind the data that were collected
O examine the facts that have been gathered
O go through all possible solutions that the group considered
O highlight the preferred solution and the reasons why
O stress the benefits of this solution in as quantified terms as possible
O detail the action needed to implement the solution
O invite questions
O agree action plan for implementation.

This tried and tested structure ensures that the audience hears what the group has to say in a logical sequence that takes them naturally from one step to the next. Group members usually choose to divide the presentation up and to tackle one or two elements each.

As far as length goes, obviously the time taken for a presentation will vary, depending upon the subject. Remembering, however, that people find it difficult to concentrate on one point for more than about 25 minutes, this should be the maximum in normal circumstances. Most presentations last between 20 and 30 minutes, followed by up to 30 minutes for questions to be asked and actions to be decided.

DEVIL'S ADVOCACY

The next vital part of preparation is for the group to be sure that it has thought of all the possible questions that could be asked, especially the awkward ones. To do this, it is useful for members to play 'devil's advocate'. This helps to raise questions that might not be considered otherwise. Members should make sure that they set aside time in preparing each management presentation to consider this aspect and to ensure that they have satisfactory answers that will convince the most sceptical of listeners.

NOTES AND VISUAL AIDS

Another aspect of preparation concerns the notes and visual aids used by speakers during the presentation. As far as notes are concerned, this is very much up to the individual to decide. The range of alternatives is very wide, from a complete word-by-word script, at one end of the spectrum, to speaking entirely from memory, at the other. In making their choice, group members should bear in mind that, although management presentations are fairly formal occasions, they are not entirely so, and from everyone's point of view the atmosphere should be as relaxed as possible. In deciding what notes to use, group members should also bear in mind that they will have visual aids, which can be very useful as a prompt. Because of this, most people choose to have notes that highlight the main headings in their presentation, rather than a complete script, but it is really up to the individual.

As far as visual aids are concerned it is much easier to generalize. A picture is worth a thousand words, or so the saying goes, and this is certainly true in the case of visual aids. We remember 10 per cent of what we hear and 50 per cent of what we see, and so the more use the group makes of the visual sense, the more likely the message is to stick. Many groups choose to show their full brainstorming lists and their Cause and Effect or Six-Word Diagrams as part of their presentation (Chapter 8), and the audience is usually very interested to see how the group has gone about tackling the problem, as well as the solution being recommended.

REHEARSAL

The final aspect of preparation concerns rehearsal. The amount of rehearsing is again something that will depend on the particular group. If members are sharing the load of presentation, it will usually be necessary at least to have a run-through to check that the handover points go smoothly. It is just as possible to over-rehearse as to do too little, however, and one run-through is usually sufficient for most presentations.

As far as preparation is concerned, therefore, it is worth remembering that half of persuasion is preparation, and that there are six aspects to be covered:

1   Establish what the group is trying to get out of the presentation.
2   Try to see things from senior management's point of view.
3   Ensure that the sequence of the presentation is logical.
4   Think through the possible awkward questions.
5   Prepare notes and visual aids.
6   Rehearse.

We can now move on and consider the meeting itself.

THE MEETING WITH MANAGEMENT

NERVES

The first important point to note is that there is likely to be a certain amount of nervousness at the beginning. This is perfectly normal, and usually helps rather than hinders, since it serves to sharpen our reflexes. Remember, however, that the group has done 80 per cent of the work before the meeting and that members have a right to be confident. Being confident and appearing so is an important part of persuasion since it shows the belief that the group has in its solutions.

FIRST IMPRESSIONS

The second point to note about the meeting is that first impressions are strongest. For this reason, the group should make quite sure that the room is set up as they want it before the meeting starts. This includes consideration of where people should sit, the positioning of the flip chart, overhead projector or computer presentation equipment, checking that the equipment works and making sure that the visual aids are in order and easy to get at. Doing this will ensure that everyone who comes realizes that they have come to an organized, well-thought-out meeting.

A further aspect of first impressions that is especially important concerns the first few words or sentences. If the group can make sure that the opening remarks are really punchy and interesting it will ensure that the attention of the audience is captured from the start. There are many ways of doing this, and the group is in the best position to decide the most appropriate choice for this particular presentation.

SELLING THE BENEFITS

The third point about the meeting is that in its presentation members should take every opportunity to sell the benefits of the solution. It is easy to imagine that the benefits are obvious to everyone, and groups need to be aware of this trap.

The three main things to consider at the meeting itself, therefore, are to:

○   be confident, remembering that 80 per cent of your work has been done before the presentation
○   remember that first impressions are especially important
○   sell the benefits of the solution.

POST-PRESENTATION

After the presentation itself, there will usually be time set aside for questions and for deciding on the action required, and the group will need to have thought through how it plans to tackle this. For example, some people prefer to have all questions answered by one nominated member, whereas others would rather anyone should speak up if they have something to say.

ACCEPTANCE

The period immediately after the presentation is also the time when it will become clear whether or not the solution proposed by the group is acceptable. If so, it is essential that members focus very carefully on what needs to happen to make sure that it gets done, and whose responsibility it is to undertake the various actions. It is all too easy to assume that events will happen automatically once the decision is made. They do not; they need people to organize and do them. Any action plan should clearly spell out the task to be done, the person or persons responsible and the time by which it will be completed.

Furthermore the plan should be written up on a flip chart or whiteboard as it is being developed so that it is there for all to see, including responsibilities and timings. This ensures that everyone has a clear picture of what has been agreed, and that nobody has any false expectations, especially about when events are going to happen. People will naturally become frustrated if they think that matters agreed upon are not being put into effect, and so agreeing the timing is vital. On this point, groups will be well advised to steer clear of the phrase 'as soon as possible' since this tends to have a different meaning for everyone who uses it.

REJECTION

Having considered what the group needs to do in the event of its proposal being accepted, it is also important that thought be given to what the reaction will be if the recommended solution is rejected. Clearly, the first response of any group in this circumstance will be one of disappointment; this is only natural. In this event, however, management should not simply say 'no'; reasons should be given to explain why it was not possible to accept the proposal at that particular time. If a problem-solving group has a proposal turned down, the members of the group must listen very actively and carefully to the reasons behind the decision, since this can help understanding and also give clues as to other alternatives that might be acceptable and which might solve all or part of the problem. It would be entirely unrealistic to expect every single solution proposed by a group to be accepted. In fact, however, there are very few outright rejections of problem-solving group proposals. That is not too surprising, since these groups solve problems in terms of facts rather than opinion.

SUMMARY

Managers and others who attend are usually very impressed with problem-solving group presentations. They find that the logical and factual way the problems are analyzed and the imaginative way the solutions are developed actually help them to say 'yes'. Opinions are easy to argue against; facts are not.

This chapter has dealt with some of the techniques in making management presentations, since there is no doubt that they are an important part of the work of problem-solving groups. This is because they represent the bridge between theoretical problem-solving activities, on the one hand, and actually getting something done, on the other. Presentations can also be fun, and perhaps the most important rule of all for group members is to enjoy them.

14

MONITORING AND EVALUATING RESULTS

It's not over 'till the fat lady sings.

The world of business is a world of change, of pressure and stress. Events happen at breakneck speed, priorities change and new problems emerge that have to be resolved. Against this background it is hardly surprising that one of the weakest areas of the problem-solving process for most groups is that of monitoring actions and evaluating results. Many groups make their presentations and then assume, usually fatally, that agreed actions will happen naturally and that the problem will remain solved for ever.

Individually and collectively we rush on to the next problem, issue and priority, oblivious to the fact that everyone else is doing the same, with the result that so often agreed actions are not put into effect and the problem creeps back to plague us again. With this in mind, it is essential that we recognize monitoring and evaluation as an essential and formal part of the problem-solving process, and accept that without it being built in, the problem should not be deemed solved.

MONITORING

Monitoring the implementation of the action plan should normally be the responsibility of the group itself, either individually or collectively, and with this in mind it is essential that an action plan is developed as a result of the management presentation. This should have not only the agreed actions, but also who will be responsible for seeing them accomplished and by when. Many groups become so immersed in their problem-solving activities, the proposed solution and their presentation to management that they quite forget that the action plan is critical to success. So often management listens attentively, is impressed by the work and agrees with the proposal but, because no action plan is agreed with timings and responsibilities, the report gets filed, lost or forgotten amongst the many other priorities and nothing actually gets done.

DO NOT ASSUME

In one organization, a group solved a problem connected with the flow of incoming materials, with an estimated benefit of £175,000 per annum. Management, as well as the group, was delighted but they fell into this trap. Being quite a large company, members of the group did not have ready access to the senior team. Over a period of months, members of the group became increasingly frustrated that nothing happened and eventually became vocal in their frustration. From being extremely positive about every aspect of the process they began to tell their colleagues that it was not worthwhile spending time becoming involved, that senior management was not interested in their ideas and that the whole process was a charade. Six months after the presentation, one of the senior team stumbled across the report of the group, wondered what had happened and was mortified to find that nothing had been done. Worse than this, attempts to recover the situation were made very difficult by the now negative response of the group members.

In the end the situation was recovered, but with considerable time and effort on the part of the senior team. The solution was finally introduced nine months after the presentation, but it was recognized that £130,000 of benefit had been lost due to this delay and staff were much more sceptical about becoming involved in new groups.

TAKE OWNERSHIP

On a more positive note, a group that solved a problem within the sales function of a medium-sized company not only agreed the implementation plan at their management presentation, but also took ownership of ensuring that it took place. They continued to meet regularly over the ensuing three-month period to report on what had been achieved and to update their action plan. This rigorous monitoring of the implementation plan ensured success and the group achieved the full benefit which they had estimated.

This amounted to a significant £112,000 in the first full year of using their solution.

EVALUATION

As far as evaluation is concerned, the group will have argued its case on the basis of the facts gathered and of a cost-benefit analysis of its preferred solutions, so it will be important for the group to review progress in the light of the predicted results. This should be done over whatever period of time is appropriate, depending on the circumstances, but should be a formal and stated part of the implementation action plan. For most issues, an updating of the evaluation should take place over about a 12-month period as a check against recurrence of the problem as well as a measure of benefits actually achieved.

One group which solved a problem with the billing process estimated a benefit of £83,000 per annum. The solution was implemented and nine months later the group reconvened to assess the impact of their work. They found that due to an increase in business in the intervening period, and another minor change that had been proposed and introduced by one group member, the actual benefit amounted to £117,000 on an annual basis. The organization had publicized the success of the group's original work through the company newsletter and had generated a lot of enthusiasm for such improvement activities. It was decided to update the story, again in the newsletter, giving thanks and recognition to the team members. This again stimulated a tremendous desire for involvement among staff at all levels. It is also worth noting that four of the seven group members were subsequently promoted, and that their willing and active participation in such improvement activities was cited as a major contributory factor in these decisions.

A less happy example involves a group that was dealing with a scheduling problem. Again the solution proposed by the group was well researched and was accepted by senior management. The solution was implemented, but when the group conducted an evaluation six or seven months later it was clear that the original problem had returned and that the benefits, which should have amounted to £84,000 per annum, were no longer forthcoming. On investigation it was discovered that insufficient explanation and retraining had been provided to those actually working the system. The result was that people reverted to 'the way we've always done it', oblivious to the fact that this was wasting money and causing significant problems to staff working further on in the process. The reaction of the staff involved, when the full story was explained, was predictable; they said 'Why didn't you explain it like that in the first place!'

EVALUATE IN QUANTIFIED TERMS

Wherever possible, the evaluation should be performed in quantitative rather than qualitative terms. In other words, there should be measurement of progress in money, time, value or any other quantifiable criterion. Less acceptable are non-quantifiable evaluations that only look at people's attitudes, communication improvement, better understanding and so on. It is not that these latter effects are unimportant, merely that they are subordinate in the work of problem-solving groups to the job of making tangible improvements in the performance of the organization.

MARKET THE RESULTS

Measured improvements, in practice, should be publicized widely through an internal marketing process that is designed to reinforce the point that problem-solving groups are concerned with action, solving problems and making sure that they stay fixed rather than coming back to haunt us again, and that everyone in the organization should be playing an active part in the process.

It is all too easy to forget these essential steps, but we do so at our peril.

SUMMARY

So many problems reoccur that in some ways it would be sensible to deem that nothing has been solved until it has not come back again for at least six months! The process of tracking solutions and making sure that action plans are indeed put into effect is critical if problems are to be solved once and for all.

PART IV
WORKING EFFECTIVELY
IN GROUPS

❖

15

WORKING TOGETHER

We must indeed all hang together, or, most assuredly, we shall all hang separately.
(Benjamin Franklin to John Hancock at the signing of the Declaration of
Independence, 4 July 1776)

This chapter is about the skills of working together effectively in
problem-solving groups. It may, at first glance, seem strange to include
such a topic in a book on problem-solving. People often assume that
we automatically know how to be good, productive members of working
groups and that no training in the subject is necessary. If we look rather
deeper than this, however, it does not seem to be so simple. Analysis of
many work groups and teams, including those with expert knowledge of the
subject in hand, indicates that very often they do not perform as well as they
might have been expected to. Nor does it seem to be any particular group
that is affected.

Committees at work have able people on them, yet they often achieve
little or nothing. Parent–teacher associations often come into destructive
conflict even though the parents and teachers involved all have the welfare
of the schoolchildren at heart. Sports club committees experience power
struggles and bad feeling, even though the people on them are perfectly able
to do the job required. So, what is it that causes these upsets? To understand
this we need to understand something called group process.

The reason why many groups have problems is not usually anything to
do with the ability of the members to understand and cope with the tasks
they are engaged in. Members of committees at work are usually very
knowlegeable and able when it comes to the technical details of the job in

hand. The same goes for sports committees, parent–teacher associations and other similar bodies. The problems that most groups encounter are largely due to their members not knowing very much about group process.

GROUP PROCESS

There is nothing mysterious or complicated about the group process; in fact, it consists of a lot of fairly simple components, many of which seem obvious once they have been explained. Rather like common sense, however, good group process is not very common, and to develop into an effective group takes time, care, effort and a desire to understand what really goes on when people get together in groups. It will be useful to start by looking more deeply into the difference between the task the group is engaged in, on the one hand, and its process, on the other.

1   The task is what the group is trying to achieve. In a problem-solving group, the task is the problem that it has been given or has decided to tackle.

2   The process consists of the means by which the group goes about achieving the task, and what influences it while doing so.

FACTORS AFFECTING GROUP PROCESS

The list of factors which can affect group process is virtually endless and so for the purpose of this chapter we shall concentrate on four of the most important areas.

Seating

One of the criteria that has most effect on how much people say, who they say it to and how much they are listened to is, strangely enough, where they are sitting in relation to the rest of the group. Getting an apparently simple matter such as this wrong can lead to individual group members feeling inhibited, unable to get into the discussion, left out, rejected. Furthermore, it never seems to be the seating arrangements that get the blame on these occasions. It always seems to be put down to such things as, 'they never did like me anyway', or 'this problem-solving thing will never work', or 'I didn't want to be here in the first place!'

Most people, if they think about it, will be able to remember a situation in a group where it seemed difficult to get involved. One of the most likely causes of this will have been that the seating arrangement was inhibiting their participation. So how should it be organized to preclude this? The basic rule about laying out a room for a problem-solving group meeting is that everyone should be able to see everyone else easily and be able to converse with them without any undue twisting and turning.

If we look at the many possible ways of laying out a room it can be seen that only the circular arrangement and the 'horseshoe' fulfil the criteria. Which of those two to choose depends upon what the group is doing at that particular meeting. If the group leader wants to conduct a training meeting, or spend most of the meeting writing on the flip chart, for example, doing a Fishbone Diagram or conducting a brainstorming meeting, the best layout for the room is likely to be the horseshoe arrangement. If the meeting is mainly a discussion, for example, working through different possible solutions to a problem, then the most appropriate layout is likely to be the circle. Investigation into the workings of groups shows quite clearly that these two ways of arranging the seating lead to more discussion involving more members of the group, and this is good from the group's point of view since it helps to get the best out of everyone.

Making sure that the seating is arranged satisfactorily will not, of course, automatically lead to everyone joining in the discussion. It will remove some of the barriers, but in many groups there will be some members who will need encouragement to give their contribution, and since these groups are about creative group problem-solving it is important that they do so. This is because, even if their thoughts may not seem important at the time, they can often spark off new ideas in the rest of the group. It should be the responsibility of all members of the group to make sure that everyone's views are heard, and this can be achieved quite simply by getting into the habit of asking for each other's contribution, rather than assuming that this will be given.

Listening

The second main area of group process, which it is important to manage, is listening. To state that the group is not likely to be very effective if the members do not listen to each other sounds so obvious as to be not worth saying. Remarkably, however, the problem of not listening or, to put it more accurately, not hearing, is probably the single biggest cause of groups not working together as effectively as they should.

The reason for this is that it is actually very difficult to hear precisely what other people mean and it is all too easy to make the wrong assumptions. Unfortunately, there is no magic wand which we can wave to make everyone listen actively and hear accurately; there would be fewer problems in life if there were. Indeed, this is a problem that cannot be fully solved but, for the group to be really effective, it needs to recognize the problem and to try to work on reducing its negative effects.

One of the best ways of helping to reduce the problem is to try to repeat what the previous speaker really meant, by using your own words. This is often much more difficult than it sounds, but it has the advantage of ensuring that other group members really do understand each other's contributions – or revealing that they do not, in which case more clarification is needed.

Building on ideas

The third area of group process which affects how well group members work together is the way the group responds to the information and ideas being put forward. There are three main aspects to this:

Win/lose First, there is the question of what is normally called win/lose. Problem-solving groups are no strangers to the idea of trying to create a situation in which everyone wins, as opposed to the more normal one where only one side can win and the other must lose. Instances of unproductive win/lose are to be seen everywhere – for example, any finger-pointing that takes place between different departments or sections is usually caused in this way. Any 'us and them' situation is likely to have its roots in win/lose and this can affect individuals as well as groups. If we are honest, most of us will be able to recollect examples of where we have rejected someone else's idea mainly because it was not our own, because we wanted to win ourselves.

Recognizing win/lose. It is actually very difficult to get out of the habit of playing the game of win/lose, but it is essential that these groups do so if they are to realize their full potential. In the light of this it will be useful to look for some rules of thumb for recognizing win/lose situations. One of the problems in diagnosing win/lose is that it is so much a part of our everyday life that it is often subconscious but, if anyone feels threatened or that they have been put on the defensive, it is likely that win/lose is at the bottom of it. Examples are, 'Oh no, Bill, anyone could see that that wouldn't work', and 'You don't really expect us to believe that nonsense, do you?'

Win/lose generally involves some sort of 'put down' which leads the person under threat to want to respond in a similar way. Possibly the best counter to occurrences of this kind is for members of the group to develop a feel for when it is present and try to warn each other. Care is needed in doing this, however, since to say, 'Jim has just made a win/lose comment', is likely to be regarded as another one! It is probably better in these circumstances to confine our observations to what our own feelings are. For example, 'I'm feeling on the defensive now'.

All of this is not to say that win/lose is always wrong, there are many areas of life where it is quite appropriate; it would be an unusual sport in which the only possible result was that both teams won! The point about win/lose, however, is that it is often negative and destructive, and it is this that members of problem-solving groups need to be on the lookout for, both in their interactions with other people in the group and their dealings with individuals and groups outside.

Finally, problem-solving groups' members should not fall into the trap of thinking that making win/lose statements is always deliberate. Very often a remark that was made quite innocently is interpreted quite differently by the receiver. If someone feels that they are in a win/lose situation then we must accept that they are, whether deliberately so or not. Because many such occurrences are accidental, however, it is often possible to clear them up simply by bringing them out into the open, rather than blaming anyone, which in its own turn is likely to start a similar reaction.

'Yes but' The way the group responds to the information and ideas put forward is also affected by what we can call the 'yes but' phenomenon. In more general sense, this has to do with whether the group tends to build on ideas or to break them down. It is easy to reject suggestions without having really thought about them. The problem is that it does not fully use the ideas of all group members. The building approach allows the group to use any ideas as a stepping-stone to achieve the best solution for the group. With this in mind it is useful to be able to recognize when the group has lapsed into breaking down ideas rather than building on them, and the words 'yes but' are a good indicator of this.

'Yes but' comments are not always negative but they are a danger signal; the group will be well advised to check when they are used. Examples of 'yes but' comments that are aimed at breaking down rather than building could include 'Yes, but we've tried that before and it didn't work', and 'Yes, but you know what they're like, they would never accept it'. The words 'yes and' are much more likely to be positive and productive, for example 'Yes, and we could collect data about the customer help line at the same time'.

Keep options open Many groups find that their final decision or solution is better if all the alternatives are kept open and considered together, rather than being rejected as they arise. This gives the group the opportunity of looking at all the possible approaches laid out in front of them, and reduces the risk of ending up implementing the last suggestion mentioned, even if no one is really committed to it. If this is the way the group wishes to work, all the possibilities should be written up on a flip chart before any discussion of their merits or disadvantages. In discussing the options once they have all been written up, members should try not to argue only for their own suggestions but to remember that the best solution is the one which best suits the group as a whole. Thinking this way will not only help to avoid win/lose, but will also help the group to arrive at the best possible answer.

Decision-making method

The fourth area of group process which it is important to cover concerns how the problem-solving group arrives at its decision. There are many possible ways in which this can be done and there are advantages and disadvantages to most of the common methods.

Majority voting Majority voting is probably the most common decision-making method of all. The main advantage of this method is that it is very quick: all that is required is a show of hands. The disadvantages of majority voting, however, are that it can lead to insufficient discussion and airing of the different views. 'Come on, let's stop talking and take a vote on it', is something that is often heard as a prelude to this method of decision-making.

A bigger problem with majority voting is that, whereas the victorious majority might be very committed to the decision, very often the losing minority feel no commitment at all, and this can be very dangerous if the decision requires the active support and backing of the whole group, as is the case in most problem-solving groups' work. There are many examples of the minority showing no commitment to the majority decision. In politics, the losing politicians and voters tend not to change their minds and support the majority party in its policies. In everyday affairs, how often do we hear people say, 'Don't blame me, I voted against it' or 'I told them it wouldn't work but they wouldn't listen'.

Silent dissenter A second decision-making mechanism, which is used more often than groups like to admit, could be called the 'consensus of silence' method. Basically, this is where someone in the group says, 'Would anyone have any objection if we did this?', or, 'Can anyone think of any reasons why we should not do that?', or 'Are there any alternative suggestions?' When no one in the group says anything, the proposal is assumed to have been agreed by everyone. The problem arises, of course, when the silence was not meant to indicate agreement, but perhaps that the group wanted time to think, or members were uninterested, bored or just could not remember what had been suggested! Probably this sounds rather far-fetched but these things all happen time and time again in different types of groups.

Loudest voice The third decision-making style we can call the loudest voice method. This method is self-explanatory and again happens very frequently. The main advantages of this style are that it is quick and final. It is a very popular method among those with loud voices and tends to be used by them all the time, but the problem, of course, is again that of the commitment of the rest of the group. This method not only applies to those who actually have the loudest voice; it equally includes situations where one person has a high degree of power or influence and uses it to get his or her own way.

Consensus Sometimes it is possible to get a completely unanimous decision, but this does not happen all that often. The next best option is to reach consensus. This is where group members try to argue for the decision which would be best for the group rather than from their own individual point of view. The consensus style of decision-making, then, is to try and reach a solution which everyone feels that they can go along with and genuinely support even though it may not be entirely their idea. The right decision with consensus is defined as the one which is best for the entire group, rather than the best for any individual or sub-group of individuals.

Consensus, therefore implies that:

- everyone is fully involved
- everyone hears and is heard
- there is substantial agreement
- there is complete commitment.

Rules for achieving consensus. Consensus is such an important decision making method that it will be of benefit to clarify the rules that will help to achieve it. These are:

- Do not just argue your own preference; be objective and logical.
- Do not change your mind simply to keep the peace; only support ideas that you can agree with, at least in part.
- Do not use conflict-reducing techniques such as voting or averaging.
- View differences of opinion as a help rather than a hindrance in coming to the best possible decision for the group.

If consensus can be achieved, it usually guarantees a high-quality decision that everyone is committed to, and so it is worthwhile trying to make it the main method in the group. The danger, however, is that it takes time and the group needs to make sure of two things. First, that the meetings do not become a talking shop. This is unlikely in practice since most group members are concerned more than anything else with action. The second danger is that consensus gets confused with compromise, when, in fact, they are very different. The problem with compromises is that very often no one is really committed to them; they represent the minimum that the individuals in the group can agree upon. Consensus, on the other hand, is the positively best solution from the point of view of the group as a whole.

This crucial difference obviously affects the quality of the decision made by the group. Consensus is quite difficult to achieve and does require considerable practice; it is, however, very rewarding since the decision which is reached is one which everyone in the group is committed to. This usually means the decision itself is a good one.

So far we have looked at four of the many aspects of group process:

○   the importance of seating arrangements
○   listening, and how difficult it is to comprehend what others really mean
○   whether the group builds on ideas or breaks them down
○   how the group arrives at decisions.

Of course, there are many more interactions occurring when people get together: they are influenced by a large variety of factors, from a person's particular mood that day to their more general likes and dislikes, strengths and weaknesses. If group members are actively conscious of the four points that have been covered, they will be looking after some of the most important areas of group process, but there will probably be a need for the group to be able to raise other points about the process of the group from time to time. Members who want to learn more about this fascinating subject will find more information in the chapter on facilitating problem-solving groups (Chapter 17).

MANAGING GROUP PROCESS

So much happens in groups that it is hard to imagine that the process will work well unless it is managed actively. Much can be achieved through careful planning and also by making sure that there are ground rules in place to cover the aspects that have been dealt with thus far. As well as this there is a requirement for a mechanism to help the group assess what actually happens in its meetings, to learn from the experience and to improve. This mechanism is called process review which again is covered in some detail in the chapter on facilitating problem solving groups. It is important at this point, however, to establish the roles and responsibilities of group members as far as managing process is concerned.

Process reviews happen in different ways. They involve an observation about what is going on in the group. It can happen spontaneously, for example, someone saying, 'Can't we get back on the subject now?' or 'If this takes much longer, I think I'll go crazy!' Alternatively the group can set aside a little time at the end of each meeting for everyone to comment very briefly on how they saw the process of the meeting.

Process review at the end of the meeting

It is always a good idea for the group to set aside 15 to 30 minutes at the end of the meeting to conduct an organized process review about what happened in the meeting, why it happened and how we can improve next time. This discipline will enable group members to develop their skill in the technique and will help the group to improve the management of its process. As the skills in process review are developed it becomes possible to agree that if someone has a constructive comment to make on the process of the group, he or she should make it when it happens. During early group meetings, however, this can be a little disruptive.

Every group member is responsible for helping to manage the process of the group. When the review takes place at the end of the meeting there will be two stages: first, gathering the views of all the members and, second, agreeing how to improve next time. The following are useful guidelines for managing this:

- Everyone must be involved, taking it in turn to give their feedback.
- Keep it brief, 1 to 2 minutes per member.
- Remember to focus on the way the group is working. Do not use the opportunity to continue working on the task.
- Comment on what was good about the meeting, what was not so good and how the group could improve next time.
- Record comments and suggestions on a flip chart or whiteboard.
- When everyone has given their feedback discuss the key issues and develop an agreed improvement plan which is recorded and circulated.
- Do not let it become an empty ritual. There are always improvements that can be made and it is up to the group to ensure that it makes them.

Typical comments that are made in process reviews include, 'I think we're listening to each other better now', or 'I feel that there are too many of us not joining in the discussion', or 'I still think that we're relying too much on Jack to come up with ideas', or 'We've really started working as a group now, rather than as a collection of individuals'.

Process review during the meeting

As we have already said, comments about process can happen spontaneously. If a member observes something which is clearly affecting the work of the group it is legitimate to call a 'time out' to share the observation and to help get the group back on track. In this eventuality it is absolutely vital that the process observation is made in descriptive rather than judgemental terms. Feedback such as, 'The trouble with you, John, is that you talk too much!' is unlikely to help. It would be more productive to say something like, 'I think it is important for everyone to have a say on this issue'.

SUMMARY

Working together in groups is by no means as easy as it is usually assumed to be. The reason for this, as we have seen, is mainly that most people do not know enough about group process. This chapter has been an introduction to this subject which should enable the group to avoid some of the pitfalls, and to help members contribute towards making their group effective and fun to work in.

16

DEALING WITH PROBLEMS IN THE GROUP

Where there's a will there's a way.

P roblem-solving groups themselves can sometimes run into problems and it is important that they are able to deal with them before they affect their work unduly. Groups have even collapsed through failing to deal with the issues that were concerning their members. This chapter is designed to explore some of the more likely types of problem that could be encountered and the recommended methods of dealing with them.

It is convenient to separate difficulties which have their roots outside the group from those which are contained within, and we shall deal first with the former.

OUTSIDE PROBLEMS

There are three main problems that can come from outside the group. First, it sometimes happens that the problem on which the group is working seems to get solved and disappear before the problem-solving cycle is completed and the group has had a chance to present its recommendations. It is as if the problem has been 'stolen' from the group. This can be both depressing and infuriating, and in these circumstances it is easy to lapse into a win/lose frame of mind. The reaction of some groups in these circumstances has been to give up and 'leave it to them'. This, fortunately, is rare. At the other end of the spectrum, some groups take a much more positive line. They claim such occurrences as successes – which they are – in the sense that often the problem would not have been solved if it were not for the work that the group had done in highlighting the problem and beginning to work on it.

THE UNKNOWN QUANTITY

What is most important if the problem does disappear, however, is that some attempt is made to understand the reason. First, it should be realized that problem-solving groups, in their early stages, are an unknown quantity. As we know from our own experience with anything new, some people want to join in straight away, others hate the idea and some prefer to see what happens before making up their minds. Very often there are questions in people's minds as to whether groups will interfere with their jobs or whether they will be a recipe for anarchy. Neither of these is the case, but in the early stages, before anyone has any experience of how the system works, it is a very understandable reaction.

It sometimes happens, therefore, that people, feeling somewhat threatened, will try to solve the problems on which the group is working. Fortunately, it does not take very long for people to realize that there is no threat, just a way of solving work problems.

ATTITUDES OUTWITH THE GROUP

The next problem which can sometimes arise from outside the group relates to the attitudes of other employees. There are usually going to be a few people who think that these groups are a waste of time, a trick, or simply a wrong way of going about things. Indeed, everyone is perfectly entitled to their view. There are occasions, however, when those who are negative about the process of improvement will make fun of those who join in. In such circumstances it is important that group members join in the fun and do not get upset. Most of the comments will be meant light-heartedly and any that are not will not be improved by standing on one's dignity.

SELF-PERCEPTION

The third difficulty that groups sometimes encounter, and occasionally create for themselves, concerns how they are seen and how they see themselves in relation to their colleagues who are not directly involved at this time. It is essential that problem-solving groups do not end up either seeing themselves or being seen as some kind of elite group, since this creates an 'us-and-them' situation among colleagues. If other people begin to see the group in this way, the members should act quickly to dispel the impression. If any member begins to think like this, we would recommend that other members of the group tackle this basic issue immediately!

With both the attitude and self-perception problems, the group should make special efforts to ensure that other interested parties know what they are doing and realize that they can contribute their ideas if they want to. This may involve informally discussing what is going on, posting up the working sheets, like Cause and Effect Diagrams, or perhaps just putting up the minutes of the meetings so that anyone who is interested can read them. Whichever methods are chosen it should be the aim of everyone involved in problem-solving groups to keep all doors open for people to be interested, to ask questions and to add their ideas if they want to.

These, therefore, are the three main problems that problem-solving groups can face from the outside. They can be solved – of that there is no doubt – given a willingness to confront them in a positive way and to avoid lapsing into finger-pointing and win/lose.

Therefore, the three main problems from the outside are:

1   At the early stage, problem-solving groups are an unknown quantity.
2   Outsiders might question the validity of the group.
3   The possibility of elitism must be avoided.

INSIDE PROBLEMS

Most groups also, at some stage or other, encounter problems from within. This is quite normal. Such difficulties need to be explored, however, and resolved if the group is to be successful.

TIME

A problem that happens occasionally is that people can get frustrated if matters do not appear to be moving quickly enough for them. The question of time perception is a difficult one. Certainly some people are more impatient than others and get frustrated when progress seems slow. The problem is that progress does take time. As we have said before, we cannot escape the need to gather data and present an organized solution based on the facts rather than opinions, and this does not happen by magic. This is merely a fact of life. This is not to say, of course, that problem-solving groups should accept that time is irrelevant. The question is, 'What is a reasonable time for events to progress?'

SEEING IT THROUGH

It is sometimes very difficult not to get impatient but many members who have been on the point of giving up have decided to see it through and found that the stimulation they get out of finally achieving the result they wanted, outweighs the frustration of waiting for it. Whilst it is obviously up to individuals to decide whether or not they leave the group, the vast majority find that it is worth while seeing through the full problem-solving cycle.

However, remember that in the early stages, a few people fall into the trap of expecting management, or someone else, to solve all the problems, when in fact it is the members who are responsible for the full problem-solving process.

MANAGING TIME-WASTING

Another problem which sometimes affects individuals or the whole group is the feeling that they are not getting anywhere and that their time is actually being wasted. Where this happens the group should allocate one of its meetings to tackling this problem, since it is likely that the solution lies in its own hands. At the meeting the group should begin by establishing that the members agree that there is a problem, and that they want to solve it and make the group successful. If this is not agreed, it is unlikely that the difficulty will be solved. Having agreed these two points, the next step is to conduct a brainstorming meeting to list all the possible reasons that the group feels might be wasting its time. During this meeting, all members should actively adopt the 'devil's advocate' role and be as critical as possible of the group and the way it has worked. By doing this, the group can give itself the opportunity to look at all the possible reasons for the problems that are in its control. Having completed the brainstorming, the group should then discuss the reasons and isolate those that are felt to be the most important causes which it is possible for the group to influence. Every attempt should be made to avoid laying the problem at anyone else's door, since this is not likely to help resolve it.

Having agreed on the reasons, the group should next develop an action plan to overcome the difficulties. Experience shows that once the key reasons have been agreed, the action needed to solve the problem is usually easy to define. The next stage is often more difficult. It involves making sure that the plan is implemented. Seeing that the changes actually occur is more difficult than defining them, and so problem-solving groups should be on their guard to ensure that they see the agreed actions through. This, of course, brings responsibility with it and one of the responsibilities problem-solving groups have is to try to be honest with themselves when problems such as this arise. It is all too easy to lapse into unproductive finger-pointing.

FAILING TO MAKE PROGRESS

There are undoubtedly occasions where groups do fail to make progress quickly enough to satisfy themselves and their sponsors. Fortunately, we know the main causes of this and so groups can diagnose their own situation and work on putting it right.

EXPERT HELP

Problem-solving groups sometimes fail to make progress in solving their problem because of a lack of relevant technical knowledge. In this case the most sensible course for the group is usually to identify people in the company who have such knowledge and invite them to help. Most experts are only too delighted to oblige and it is surprising on how many occasions an occurrence such as this has improved the working relationships between the areas concerned.

MOTIVATION

The group may also fail to progress, not so much for want of technical help, but because members feel that they are losing motivation. This is likely to happen occasionally with any group, and the best response in these circumstances is for the group to lay the problem to rest for a week, and to come back to it with a fresh mind at the next meeting. This might involve the group in cutting short one of its meetings, or perhaps going on to another less important problem, but either way it is usually more satisfactory than becoming stale with the problem.

STRESSED RELATIONSHIPS

Problem-solving groups can also sometimes have problems when relationships between members appear to become stressed. Fortunately, this does not happen very often but, when it does, it obviously needs to be tackled urgently. In fact, it is remarkable how often problems which appear to be about relationships are actually about other matters.

Research that has been done on organizations and groups indicates that where relationships appear to be a problem there are actually four potential causes. They are:

1   Confusion over what the group is trying to achieve.
2   Problems over roles in the group.
3   Confusion over procedures or the way the group works.
4   True interpersonal difficulties.

It is perhaps surprising that this list is in decreasing order of importance.

This is to say, most of the problems that occur are those about objectives and roles rather than relationships.

GOAL CONFUSION

Any group that feels it has problems of relationships should therefore check first whether the difficulty really is owing to this or something else. The recommended method to tackle this is for the group members first of all to state individually what it is that they want to achieve from the group in general and the particular problem being tackled at the moment. These should be written up on a flip chart as two separate lists. Members should then clarify any of the statements of goals and can go on to discuss the differences between individuals. It is surprising how often this can lead to an increase of mutual understanding and a dramatic reduction in the tension that the group was experiencing earlier. If this does not appear to be the cause of the difficulty, however, the group should go on to consider the problem of roles.

ROLES

When we talk about roles in a group we are talking about the 'jobs' people do while the group is meeting. It may seem strange to talk about 'jobs' in this context, but it is a useful way of looking at how groups operate. There are many different roles which can be performed in a group. Some of them are useful and productive, while others hinder the work of the group. One important role is that of the leader.

Leadership

Quite often, groups experience problems if either the leadership is not adequate, or if another member of the group tries to undermine or take over from the leader. Fortunately, this does not happen too often with problem-solving groups but, where it does, it is important that the issue is brought out into the open and talked about, since if it is just left it is likely to impair the work of the group seriously.

Gatekeepers

Another important role in effective groups is called 'gatekeeping'. This describes the person who makes sure that everyone in the group gets a chance to speak. Virtually every group has people who speak a lot and those who do not say very much, but it is essential, if the group is to be effective, that everyone's opinion be taken into account, so, making sure this happens is an important task. Group members should ask themselves whether anyone is fulfilling this role in the group, since, if no one is, the consequences can be not only that the quality of the group's work declines, but also that relationships in the group can become strained.

Devil's advocate

The role of devil's advocate is once again important. Without it, the group can be led into compromises that nobody really agrees with. The devil's advocate role is a slightly dangerous one, though, in that it can cause unnecessary upset among the group members if it is not handled appropriately. The most likely problem here lies in giving feedback which is seen as being too judgemental. There is a big difference between saying, 'That's a load of rubbish, John, we should set up the system on a trial basis first', and 'An alternative that we should consider as well is to set up the new system on a trial basis first'. This is more than simply playing with words, since if a message is rejected by someone because they see it as being too aggressive and critical, the message is ineffective and does not help the group to move forward.

In tackling problems such as this it is essential that the problem-solving group members who see the difficulty do not fall into the same trap and become too judgemental themselves. It is much better in circumstances like these to describe how you felt; for example, 'Maybe it's just me, but when you said that, John, I felt as though I was being treated like a fool'. This allows John to see the effect he has had and to do something about it if he wants to. If, on the other hand, we say, 'You tried to make a fool out of me', the usual response would be, 'No, I didn't'. The difficulty with this is that it rarely leads to the solution of the problem.

DOMINANT MEMBERS

Occasionally, groups meet the problem of one of the members being too dominating and trying to force his or her wishes on the group. This can be quite difficult to deal with because sometimes it is hard to get a word in edgeways! In circumstances like this there is a danger of setting up a win/lose situation between the person concerned and some or all of the rest of the group, and this, of course, should be avoided at all costs. Probably the best course of action is to suggest going round the room in turn so that everyone's views are heard. This gives a structure to work within which can be useful. If the domineering person interrupts, it should be emphasized that the way problem-solving groups work is for everyone's ideas to be heard and thus it is important to complete the round. If the problem persists, then the offender should be given feedback about the effect of his or her behaviour. This, again, is a situation in which it is better to describe our own feelings; for example, 'I'm feeling frustrated at the moment because I don't feel I'm being given the opportunity to listen to everyone's point of view'. By expressing our feelings in this way we can avoid the kind of win/lose situation which is almost inevitable if we say, 'Don't you ever stop talking!' or something of a similar nature.

In general, the key to dealing with situations when someone is adversely affecting the work of the group is to tackle them by describing how we are feeling as a result of the particular behaviour, and by avoiding making judgements about anyone, since this almost invariably ends up as a win/lose situation.

GROUP PROCEDURES

If the roles do not seem to be the problem, the next area to look at is the procedures being used by the group, i.e., the way the group works. There are a number of questions the group needs to ask itself in order to explore this. First, the decision-making method should be checked and its effect on members of the group discussed. For example, the group may have lapsed into majority voting, leaving the minority unhappy and uncommitted.

If the decision-making arrangements are felt to be satisfactory, another procedural issue to be discussed is the style of communication in the meetings. For example, does everyone end up talking at once? Or are the meetings so tightly controlled that they are stilted and uncomfortable? Sometimes groups can slip into ways of communicating that cause problems between some or all of the members. The next question to be asked is whether there is an agreed agenda for each meeting and, furthermore, does the group tend to stick to it or does it drift on to other topics unrelated to the matter in hand?

Finally, do members do what they say they are going to do, or do agreed actions get delayed and forgotten? Also, how does the group react if this is the case? Is it just accepted without comment, or are the reasons why discussed? Do the reasons sound like excuses, or are they valid?

RELATIONSHIPS

If relationships are the real problem, the best way of tackling the issue is for those concerned to meet outside the group and talk it through. Fortunately such occurrences are rare, but when they do occur it is usually sensible to ask a facilitator to sit in on the discussion, since an outsider can often 'see the wood for the trees', while those involved cannot.

Some of the questions, therefore, that need to be asked to explore whether the group has a problem with the way it works are about:

O objectives
O roles
O procedures
O relationships.

SUMMARY

This chapter has covered some of the main difficulties problem-solving groups can experience. They do not occur frequently, but it is important to remember that the best groups do have their problems. What makes them the best is that they can tackle the problems successfully. No group should feel that it has failed in any way if it comes up against any of these difficulties. The focus should be very much on being successful in dealing with them. This can be attempted by the group itself or with the aid of a facilitator. Again, there is no slur involved in asking for help; there are times when only an outsider can see what is really going on. It is far better to ask for help than to have the group get into real difficulties and run the risk of collapsing.

 Whatever problems the group encounters, it is more likely to solve them if all the members work together, and are of a common mind in both wanting to solve them and being confident of the group's ability to do so. With this attitude virtually every problem can be overcome. We can all win!

17

FACILITATING PROBLEM-SOLVING GROUPS

❖

Judge not that you be not judged.

The role of facilitator is a key one in assisting the success of problem-solving groups, but only, of course, if it is performed knowledgeably and with skill. At its root it is a developmental role and the main issues that should concern anyone involved in this way are covered in this chapter.

The job of the facilitator of problem-solving groups is, first, to help them to be successful and, second, to develop them to become independent of the need for facilitative support. In practice this initially will usually involve the facilitator in a training capacity and will always include helping groups to understand and deal with what is happening in their meetings that is either helping or hindering their progress.

It is important at the outset, however, to reiterate that the primary function is to develop the knowledge and skills needed for groups to be successful and self-sufficient; it is not to solve the problem the group is working on, neither is it to lead the group nor to become a de facto member.

Facilitators attend the meetings of the groups that they are working with until they reach the desired state of independence. Their role within the meetings will vary as a result of the levels of knowledge and skill of the leader and members, and also the dynamics of the particular meeting.

Facilitators also have the important tasks of working with the leader to plan the meeting and to review it with the leader afterwards. So the cycle could be described as – plan, do, review.

139

THE FACILITATOR AS TRAINER

For problem-solving groups to be successful they need to use the problem-solving process rigorously. First, this involves understanding the steps in the overall design and the reasons for them. Second, it requires that group leaders and their members know how to use the different problem-solving techniques properly. This requires training, of this there is no doubt. There are two main approaches to meeting this requirement.

Most people are not particularly adept at learning things in theory and then applying them at a later date. It has often been said that we remember approximately 10 per cent of what we hear, 50 per cent of what we see and 80 per cent of what we do. Because of this, simply sending people on problem-solving training courses would not seem to be a particularly good way of equipping them to be able to use the process successfully in practice. Indeed it is not, unless additional support in the shape of a facilitator is provided to work with the group as it engages in problem-solving activities. The advantage of this approach, however, is that those involved will have been through the different stages and techniques in their training and will recall them quickly with less help than might otherwise have been needed. If this method is used, the role of the facilitator working with the group will usually be to remind the members of the particular technique that is to be used in the particular meeting, to summarize the steps and to ensure that the group uses them rigorously.

The alternative approach is for the facilitator, working with the leader, to use the first part of a meeting to train members in the particular technique that is to be used during the rest of the meeting. This way of handling the need ensures that people immediately get the chance to put their learning into practice, and so reinforce it in the most powerful way.

Both approaches have their merits and which one to use will depend on individual circumstances. The only absolute is that training and support in the proper use of the overall process and the techniques within it are provided to any problem-solving group. This must continue until such point that the skills have become ingrained and the process has become simply the normal way that problems are dealt with in the organization.

TASK AND PROCESS

The second major responsibility of the facilitator is to understand the difference between task and process, and to know enough about process to be able to help the group to manage its meetings well.

Many people have expressed their disbelief about groups and how ineffective they so often are. One said, 'Put a group of sane people in a room, give them a task, and you end up with collective madness'.

The fact is that 95 per cent of the difficulties that lead to ineffective working in groups are problems to do with an apparent inability of members to manage the way they work together, the process. The vast majority of people in groups have the technical knowledge required for them to play their part in the particular task; they are selected for the group on this basis. What they lack is knowledge and skill in the process. The job of the facilitator is to assist in this by equipping groups with the knowledge and skills they need to make them effective.

The subject of what happens in groups, group dynamics, is vast. Thousands of books have been written on different aspects of it. In this chapter we will focus on the key elements which the facilitator needs to know and to understand as far as problem-solving groups in organizations are concerned. In summary these are:

O   the normal stages that groups go through
O   individual roles and the balanced team
O   what to look for in groups.

We will then consider the main ways of helping groups to manage process:

O   process review at the end of meetings
O   process observation during meetings.

Finally we will summarize the key behaviours that are directly:

O   facilitative
O   action oriented.

STAGES OF GROUP DEVELOPMENT

Groups that meet on a regular basis, such as problem-solving groups, go through a number of stages of their development. This is a well-researched phenomenon and it is important that we are able to identify the stages and deal with the issues that arise out of each of them.

Probably the best known model was proposed by Tuckman who identified four distinct phases that he called Forming, Storming, Norming and Performing. For the practising facilitator, however, a more useful approach distinguishes between what is happening in the relationships among group members and what is happening concerning the task at each stage the group goes through. This way of viewing the subject was developed by John E. Jones who co-founded University Associates and was instrumental in the development and use of structured experiences in training. It does not conflict with Tuckman's interpretation, indeed, the broad stages are much the same, but it is more useful because of the distinction that is made between relationships and task issues.

STAGE 1: DEPENDENCY AND ORIENTATION

A group's life at the outset is characterized on the personal relations side by a phase of 'dependency'. Group members, because they have been thrust into a new situation which creates anxiety, and a little confusion, will tend to lean on the leader or facilitator to give them clear guidance about what the ground rules are, to set the agenda and to provide leadership. They will be quite defensive in their own behaviour and will avoid taking what they see as risks in what they do and say.

On the task side at this first stage there will be a considerable amount of questioning from members about why they are here, what are they supposed to do, what are their goals. Members are trying to get themselves 'oriented' within this new setting.

This phase, clearly, is unlikely to be very productive. It need not, and probably will not, last long but the facilitator needs to understand that it will happen, if for no other reason than to be able to reassure members that it is quite normal.

STAGE 2: CONFLICT AND ORGANIZATION

On the relations side of the equation this stage is about emerging 'conflict'. Members become a bit more comfortable and start to express their own agendas. They will be more willing to criticize others, to question motives and to challenge the leadership of the group. They may, as well, begin to try to use the group as a platform for their whims which can quickly distract the group from its purpose. Others may feel resentment and withdraw so it can be seen that the conflict is not necessarily overtly apparent, but it is there.

The task side of this stage is one of 'organization'. Because members are beginning to 'flex their muscles' questions will be raised about responsibilities, the rules and boundaries of the task to be accomplished and the level of authority of the group. Because views about such matters are likely to be different there is the likelihood of more interpersonal conflict which must be resolved before the group can move on.

Again this is not a particularly comfortable or productive period and again it is important for the facilitator to be aware that it will happen and to have the skills to move the group quickly through it. It is also worth recognizing that on the task side some important aspects will be dealt with at this stage, and from the relations point of view it is better to confront these issues properly now rather than have them emerge again later when it would be more damaging to the effective working of the group.

STAGE 3: COHESION AND DATA-FLOW

Stage three of the life cycle of any group is altogether more positive and fruitful. Group members feel positive about having resolved the conflicts that arose during stage two. There is a feeling of togetherness which is comfortable and rewarding in its own right and so on the personal relations front it is not surprising that this is the stage of 'cohesion' during which common, rather than individual, goals can be explored openly and agreed.

From the point of view of the task rapid progress can be made because members are much more willing to be open with each other, to share information and to work together productively. The situation is one where the 'data-flow' is opened up.

There is no doubt that this is a productive phase but there is a danger that members feel so good about themselves, and each other, that they begin to forget why they are there, which is to complete a task, because their needs are being fulfilled by being a part of a comfortable, cohesive group. We have all come across groups that meet regularly, have enjoyable meetings yet produce nothing. They exist in almost every organization.

STAGE 4: INTERDEPENDENCE AND PROBLEM-SOLVING

The final phase of group development is not achieved by many but it is well worth striving for as it represents the pinnacle of successful group working. On the relations side this stage is characterized by real 'interdependence' where members are committed to the team and its shared goals rather than on their own. Members will happily share the leadership of the group, influenced by the topic or the particular skills required. They will work in whatever way helps the group most, whether it be in sub-groups, individually or as an entity. They are not a group of individuals, they are a team in the true and complete sense of that word.

On the task side the focus can now be on real problem-solving. The group will explore new ideas and approaches that might help them to be more effective. They are justifiably confident of their ability to work effectively together and to deliver results. Personal agendas are a thing of the past; the success of the team in terms of what it delivers is the key for every member.

Knowledge about these predictable phases is important for the facilitator who can then help groups through the uncomfortable first two stages, can assist groups in avoiding the dangers of the third phase whilst helping them to recognize their achievements, and, if fortunate enough to observe it, can sit back and admire any group that achieves the fourth stage!

Finally, it is worth remarking that facilitators who show a willingness, even an appetite, for having their views challenged will assist the group in moving through these stages since it will help to establish a norm of open and honest communication more quickly than otherwise would be the case.

TEAM ROLES

To understand what is happening in groups and to be able to assist them more effectively as facilitators it is important to be able to recognize the different roles being played by members and also to be able to assess the balance of the group in terms of the roles which are needed to help it function successfully. The most useful system for doing this is that proposed by Belbin, and facilitators will do well to include it in their work.

As a result of his research into effective and ineffective groups Belbin identified eight 'team roles' and found that any individual was unlikely to be dominant in more than two. He also concluded that the best groups were balanced in that they contained members who, between them, covered all the roles. There are various ways of establishing a person's team roles, one of which is a readily available self-marking questionnaire. Alternatively visit www.dulewicz.com

The team roles Belbin identified and the characteristics attributed to them are as follows.

COMPANY WORKER

The company worker is conservative, disciplined and reliable. This is the person who organizes things and who turns ideas and plans into practical forms of action. The company worker would say things like:

- ○ 'Let's write it up on the flip chart.'
- ○ 'We could do that within our budget.'
- ○ 'Given the time we've got we could ...'

CHAIRPERSON

The chairperson is mature, confident and trusting, the person who clarifies goals and priorities and motivates colleagues. The chairperson would say:

- ○ 'What we are here to do is ...'
- ○ 'To summarize, the main points seem to be ...'
- ○ 'Let's do this first and then move on to that.'

SHAPER

The shaper is highly strung, outgoing and dynamic. Shapers challenge, pressurize and find a way round obstacles. Typical shaper comments would include:

- ○ 'We're wasting time, we should ...'
- ○ 'No, you're wrong, the main issue is ...'
- ○ 'If we put what you've said with the other suggestion we could ...'

PLANT

The plant is clever, imaginative and unorthodox. This is the person who creates original ideas and solves difficult problems. Plants would say:

- ○ 'Turning that on its head gives us ...'
- ○ 'Let's look at it from a different angle.'
- ○ 'A good idea would be ...'

RESOURCE INVESTIGATOR

The resource investigator is extrovert, enthusiastic, curious and communicative. Resource investigators explore new possibilities, develop contacts and negotiate. Typical comments would include:

- ○ 'What a great idea.'
- ○ 'I know someone who can.'
- ○ 'Don't worry, I can get them.'

MONITOR/EVALUATOR

The monitor/evaluator is sober, intelligent, dry and objective. This is the person who sees all the options, analyzes and judges likely outcomes accurately. The monitor/evaluator would say:

- ○ 'We have to watch out for ...'
- ○ 'Let's not overlook ...'
- ○ 'The problem with that is ...'

TEAM WORKER

The team worker is social, mild, accommodating and perceptive. This is someone who listens, builds on ideas, averts friction and handles difficult people well. Team workers say:

- ○ 'There's no need to fight about it.'

O   'Let's listen to Jim's idea.'
O   'Sally, why don't you explain that a bit more?'

COMPLETER/FINISHER

The completer/finisher is painstaking, conscientious and anxious. They search for errors, omissions and oversights. They focus on and keep others to schedules and targets. Typical comments would include:

O   'You can't do that, we'll be a week late.'
O   'Let me check that.'
O   'We have to do this if the whole thing is going to work.'

Practising facilitators can provide a good service to the groups they work with by considering the balance of team roles that is apparent and by encouraging members to work hard to fill any gaps, since there is clear evidence that all the roles have an important part to play if the group is to be really successful.

WHAT TO LOOK FOR IN GROUPS

One of the main things a facilitator does is to observe behaviour in the group and to diagnose its effectiveness or otherwise in helping the group to achieve its goals. We can consider the important influences that individuals have on group process under the following main headings. Facilitators can use the questions to aid their diagnosis of what is actually happening in groups that they are working with and to encourage the group to do the same.

ACTIVITY LEVEL

In any group there will be an unequal level of participation among the members. Some will be active, others will be quieter. The balance will often change during the course of a meeting. In some groups progress seems to depend on one or two individuals and we need to know why this is and what effect it is having on the other members.

1   Who are the high participators?
2   Who are the low participators?
3   Are there any shifts in participation? Why is this?
4   Are the more active participants monopolizing the discussion?
5   How are the quieter people treated? How is their silence interpreted? Consent? Lack of interest? Disagreement?

6   Who talks to whom? Is there any reason for this?
7   Who keeps the ball rolling? Why and how?

KINDS OF INFLUENCE

The level of participation is not always the same as the level of influence. Quite often people who talk a lot are not really listened to, and have little influence on the group and vice versa. Some people try to force their own opinions on the group, others prefer a more democratic style and want to make sure that everyone has a say. Some individuals may even try to influence the group by refusing to be drawn in.

Questions the facilitator can pose concerning influence in the group are:

1   Who are the influential group members?
2   Why is this? Is it because of their knowledge of the subject or for other reasons? What are the other reasons?
3   Which members are low in influence? Is there any shifting in levels of influence? If so, why?
4   What styles of influence are used in the group, for example autocratic, democratic, laissez-faire? Which are accepted and which are rejected by other group members?
5   Do the styles of influence of the dominant members fit in with the desire and expectation of the rest of the group or is a win/lose relationship developing between different people on the basis of the style of influence being used?

DEFENSIVENESS

We all have defence mechanisms and use them from time to time to avoid having to confront what is really happening. They often operate at the subconscious level, which can make them difficult to deal with since any direct feedback is likely to be rejected. Despite this it is important that we are able to identify them and that we develop the skills to be able to deal with them as they can seriously undermine the working of the group.

As far as individuals are concerned the most common defence mechanisms are as follows:

1   Rationalization. This is the substitution of a false reason for the real one to avoid having to cope with the implication of the real reason. For example someone might say, 'The reason the presentation didn't go well was that the projector bulb broke', rather than, 'We didn't have a spare bulb and we didn't perform well'.
2   Withdrawal. Sometimes this can be seen as a physical withdrawal, for example, someone moves their chair back or sits back, or even

leaves the room. On other occasions signs of obvious boredom and refusal to join in can be seen as defensive reactions.

3   Cynicism. This is often characterized by questioning the validity of the group or whether its work is worthwhile, for example, 'It's not worth the effort, they'll just say no in the end'. Someone who reacts like this could be feeling defensive about their ability to work effectively in such a problem-solving group.

4   Generalization. At times we all use generalizations rather than being specific and they are often defence mechanisms. Someone who was worried about playing a part in a presentation to senior management could say, 'I'm not sure presentations should be part of our work because people can get quite anxious about them'.

5   Competition. Competition within the group, either between members or with the leader or facilitator is a common phenomenon, especially in the early stages of the group's life.

As has already been stated we are all defensive to a greater or lesser degree. For the facilitator the challenge is to see the behaviour and to assess it in the context of the group and its work. So key questions here are:

1   Is this really what the group member wanted to say or do or are there other circumstances to explain the behaviour?

2   Is the defensive behaviour having a detrimental effect on the working of the group? If not, let it pass.

DECISION-MAKING PROCEDURES

Many decisions are made in groups without considering their effect on other members. Some people try to impose their own will while others wish to involve everyone in everything.

1   Does anyone make 'self-authorized' decisions without checking them out with other members? What effect does this have on the group?

2   Does the group drift from topic to topic? Who does this? Why does it happen?

3   Who supports the suggestions of others? Does this support lead to sub-grouping and the manipulation of the group?

4   Is there evidence of a majority pushing decisions through against the will of the minority? Is voting used and if so what effect does it have especially on the minority?

5   Is there any attempt to get all members involved in a decision that everyone can support? What effect does this have on the group?

6   Do people make contributions that are ignored? What effect does this have on those involved?

TASK FUNCTIONS

Any problem-solving group needs to be concerned with getting the job done. There are a range of behaviours which are helpful in this.

1   Does anyone ask for or make suggestions about the best way to proceed or to tackle a problem?

2   Does anyone attempt to summarize what has been covered or what has been going on in the group?

3   How much do members ask for facts, ideas, opinions or feelings?

4   Who keeps the group on target? Who prevents topic-jumping or going off at tangents?

MAINTENANCE FUNCTIONS

These are behaviours that affect the tone and morale of the group. When they are positive they help to maintain good and harmonious working relationships and to create an atmosphere which encourages people to contribute.

1   Who helps quieter members to get into the discussion?

2   Who cuts off others or interrupts them?

3   How well are members getting their ideas across? Does anyone try to help others to clarify their ideas?

4   How are ideas rejected? How do people react when their idea is not accepted? Does anyone provide support when someone's ideas are rejected?

GROUP ATMOSPHERE

The overall 'feel' of a group will influence its effectiveness. Different people like their groups to have different characteristics so there is no one right atmosphere, but whatever it is it needs to work positively for the particular group.

1   Who seems to prefer a friendly, congenial atmosphere? Is there any supression of conflict or unpleasant feelings?

2   Who seems to prefer an atmosphere of conflict and disagreement? Do any members provoke and annoy others?

3   Do members seem involved and interested? How would you describe the atmosphere? For example, is it one of work, play, satisfaction, avoidance, boredom, excitement?

MEMBERSHIP

A major concern of members concerns the degree to which they feel accepted by and included in the group. Often sub-groups can develop which can be very debilitating for the group overall especially because they are often based on win/lose.

1   Is there any evidence of sub-grouping? Sometimes two or three members either consistently support each other or continually disagree.
2   Is there a sub-group that is vying for leadership? If so, is one person behind it?
3   Do the same sub-groups always form over the same issues?
4   Do some people seem to be 'insiders' and others 'outsiders'? How are the 'outsiders' treated?
5   Are any sub-groups hindering the work of the group? Is the group in control of this aspect of its process?
6   Is there any straightforward 'ganging-up'? If so it must be confronted quickly.

FEELINGS

During any group discussion feelings are generated by the interaction between members. Feelings, however, are not often talked about. Perhaps the only clues we have are non-verbal ones yet the existence of positive or negative feelings have a major effect on the working of the group, so it is important to observe this aspect closely.

1   What signs of feelings do you observe? Are they ones of anger, irritation, frustration, warmth, excitement, boredom, defensiveness?
2   Do you see any attempt by some members to stop the expression of feelings, especially negative ones? How is this done? Does anyone do it consistently? What effect does it have?

NORMS

Standards or ground rules will emerge in any group. They are often unspoken and can help or hinder the work of the group. These norms, certainly the explicit ones, usually express the beliefs or desires of most of the group members as to the way the group should operate.

1   What are the explicit rules that members agree to abide by?
2   What sanctions does the group impose on members who violate these norms? Are the sanctions productive or not?

3   What seem to be the unspoken rules? Would it help to make these explicit?

4   Are certain topics avoided? Who seems to reinforce this avoidance? How do they do it? Does this avoidance have any real effect on the working of the group?

5   Are members overly nice and polite to each other? Are only positive feelings expressed? Do people agree too readily? What happens when there is disagreement?

6   Are members able to probe each other about their feelings?

7   Do questions tend to be restricted to intellectual topics or events outside the group?

8   Do any of the unspoken norms contravene any of the core principles of effective group working?

There is no doubt that the practising facilitator needs at least a working knowledge of the factors that influence and make up what we have called group process. This is needed so that the group can be helped towards maturity and success in managing this vital aspect of working in groups.

PROCESS REVIEW

The mechanism used by groups for managing process is called process review. This can be done in a number of ways, and virtually always requires the help and support of the facilitator until the group is self-sufficient in the skills and disciplines that are needed to do it well. This is one of the most vital roles of the facilitator because it is highly unlikely that groups will conduct process reviews unless they are encouraged to do so, yet it is the single most important factor in determining how successful they will be in their work.

The idea of process review is that the group is active in trying to understand the factors that affect the way that it is working with a view to improving its performance. This is important since good, well-managed group process is the route to successful task accomplishment.

There are two main ways of handling the requirement.

PROCESS REVIEW AFTER A MEETING

Immediately following every group meeting a period of 15 to 30 minutes should be set aside to conduct a process review. Until members get used to the discipline the facilitator should start by introducing the purpose of the session, which is to:

O   understand what was happening during the meeting

O   learn from this
O   set goals for improvement.

It should also be reinforced that the subject is process, that is, the way that we have worked together, and that members should not use this time to continue working on the problem that the group is engaged in trying to solve.

The facilitator, from having observed the meeting, will probably have a number of points to put in front of the group, but it is important first that the views of the members are collected and listened to. The most usual way of handling this is to invite each member in turn to give their views about:

O   the most important things about the way we worked together that
       helped the meeting
O   the most important things about the way we worked together that
       hindered the meeting
O   what would help us to improve at the next meeting.

The facilitator should record the main points made on a flip chart or whiteboard. It is best to do this as three separate lists.

Before inviting peoples' views, however, it is important to lay down a few rules, which should be posted so that everyone can see them. These rules can be adapted to suit the group but should include the following:

O   Everyone should contribute.
O   Keep it short, say 2 minutes per person for the initial round up.
O   Describe what you felt or thought rather than judging people or
       motives.
O   Listen and do not interrupt.

After everyone has had their initial say the facilitator needs to decide on the best way of gaining agreement to an improvement plan that will help the group but that is not so daunting that it leads to members becoming demoralized. If there is widespread agreement from the 'round robin' about what needs to be done, this could be simple. On other occasions there will be less agreement and it may well be that group members have not included some key points picked up by the facilitator.

In these circumstances the next step is for the facilitator to add observations to the lists of member comments and to explain them to the group. Once this has been done members should be encouraged first to ask questions for clarification and then to discuss, in a controlled way, the most important things that they could do to improve the process of the group in the future.

At the outset it will be wise for the facilitator to reinforce the importance of improvement rather than simply accepting the status quo, and to give appropriate encouragement and recognition when the group sets itself improvement targets and works towards their achievement.

However it is done, facilitators will need to use their skills to achieve an agreed action plan, which should be recorded on the flip chart or whiteboard for all to see. After the meeting the plan should be circulated to members to act as a reminder and should be reviewed and reinforced at the start of the next meeting.

PROCESS OBSERVATION DURING A MEETING

The ideal situation is one where groups have the understanding and the skills to manage process whilst working on the task. This can be developed, and indeed should be the goal of the facilitator, but it tends to take time and a 'softly, softly' approach is probably the best.

A process observation is an observation that is made during the meeting that concerns the way the group is working. Sometimes they are spontaneous comments that may not be helpful, especially if they are judgemental. The idea of this kind of intervention, however, is more controlled. Process happens all the time and there is a lot of it. It is difficult for everyone to keep track of what is really going on that may be harming the group. However, an individual member might spot something of importance and, rather than wait until the end of the meeting to mention it, may think that it is better to deal with it at the time. In this circumstance the procedure to use is for that person to call a short 'time out' to make a process point which the group must listen to. Only points which are having a significant impact on the group should be the subject of such interventions, since raising trivial issues during the meeting will do more harm than good. Typically valid process observations will concern such things as:

○   more than one meeting going on
○   obvious examples of members not listening to each other
○   not allowing people to finish what they are saying.

Another valid subject would be if any of the problem-solving techniques were being used inaccurately or inappropriately.

Overall, then, a primary task of the facilitator is to develop the group to a stage where they are able and willing to manage the process of their meetings actively and successfully. In this section we have dealt with some of the key aspects of knowledge and skill that are needed to bring this to pass.

EFFECTIVE FACILITATIVE BEHAVIOURS

The main task of the facilitator in the context of this book is to equip problem-solving groups with the knowledge and skills they need to be able to continue their problem-solving work unaided. As has already been discussed, this will involve training groups in the problem-solving process and specific techniques, and in helping groups to manage the way that they work, their process. For this to be achieved effectively any facilitator requires a knowledge of the key behaviours that are known to assist in this kind of work.

Research indicates that there are a number of behaviours that are directly facilitative whilst others are likely to lead to effective action by the group, which as we know is the main purpose of the role.

FACILITATIVE BEHAVIOURS

There are four behaviours that have been found to be particularly facilitative in their effect.

Empathy

The first behaviour that is directly facilitative is creating empathy. Without the feeling that the facilitator is 'on the same wavelength' it will be hard to achieve the desired result and the relationship between the facilitator and the group can deteriorate into a rather shallow, sterile, game-playing charade.

Empathy breeds a feeling of comfort and confidence that leads, in turn, to a greater willingness to be open in both giving and receiving feedback. Empathy is not just a 'chemical' reaction between people, it can be developed if the facilitator knows how. Some of the things that can be done are relatively straightforward, for example, observing the body language of the other party and 'mirroring' it in a subtle way. Another powerful tool lies in talking the same 'language' as the other party, by which we mean that some people talk in terms of their feelings – if so, use the same type of language. Others use different types of words, 'I think we should …', 'It's clear that …'; again, if this is the case, use the same kind of language.

Specificity

It is relatively easy to discuss issues in broad and general terms, we all do it all of the time, for example we say, 'Everyone knows that …'. Everyone in the world, or just some of them? We often use generalizations to 'fudge' issues because it is less demanding than being specific, but this method does not help very much if our goal is to help people and groups to identify and work successfully on defined improvement opportunities.

From the facilitator's point of view it is important to avoid using such generalizations and to be specific when working with groups. Equally, when faced with generalizations from others it is useful and facilitative to get the other party to be more precise. So, using the above example, when someone says, 'Everyone knows that …' the facilitator could ask, 'Who, precisely, knows that …'.

Genuineness

The third generic facilitative behaviour is genuineness. If the people that we are working with doubt our genuineness they are very unlikely to be open and the relationship is likely to evaporate into a series of meaningless platitudes, if it continues at all. The judgement of our genuineness, from the point of view of those we are dealing with, will tend to be made on two counts. First, are we seen as being genuinely interested in the groups we are working with on their own terms, and prepared to deal with them on this basis and, second, are we interested in their success or our own self-aggrandizement? Of course these judgements will be made on the basis of the perceptions of group members and may well be erroneous in our eyes. They will, however, be believed by those that develop them and this should alert us to the importance of this issue.

Respect

The final behaviour in the list of specifically facilitative behaviours is respect. There is little doubt as to the importance of this ingredient. Facilitators, by the very nature of the relationship they have with the groups they work with, have no organizational 'power' to fall back on. The success of what they do depends on the relationship they build with groups and their members.

Respect, of course, is generated differently in different circumstances and the wise facilitator will consider what is likely to engender this precious ingredient with each and every group and individual. It will often come down to quite simple things such as do you wear business attire or don't you (either could be right). Importantly, facilitators should observe and listen to those that they are working with since this will invariably reveal what is valued and respected. Finally, manner, demeanour, politeness and a genuine interest and enthusiasm are always valuable ingredients.

ACTION-ORIENTED BEHAVIOURS

As facilitators we are interested that the groups we work with achieve results rather than simply have congenial meetings that produce nothing, so the four behaviours that are likely to lead to constructive action are of particular interest.

CONCRETENESS

In trying to help groups to become effective it will not help very much if what we say and recommend is vague and woolly. Equally, it will not help if we allow them to be the same. In developing action plans with our groups we need to be aware of the need for them to state what they intend in concrete terms. If we accept vagueness, it is highly likely that any action will be vague in itself, which will be frustrating for all concerned.

IMMEDIACY

The idea of giving up a bad habit, say smoking, is easy if the plan is to stop next month or next year. If an action is agreed to be achieved in six months it is unlikely to receive a very high priority. Most likely it will never happen. The fact is that the more immediate the requirement the more likely it is to create action. This does not mean that everything has to be done immediately, but it should be realized, in today's turbulent world, that things that are scheduled for more than about a month hence will often be lost amongst everything else that has to be done. For some of us even a week is long term! If there are things that will take time it is sensible to break them down into 'bite-sized chunks' some of which can be actioned quickly. A useful role of the facilitator is to help groups to make at least some of their work and actions immediate.

POSITIVE CONFRONTATION

Inevitably there will be times when facilitators have to work with people who are less willing to become involved and to play their part than others in the group. There will also be occasions when this becomes an issue that needs to be dealt with before it begins to have a wider effect. Having tried other approaches there will be times when direct confrontation of the issue is the only remaining strategy. If this is to work though, the nature of the confrontation must be positive. Facilitators in this situation will need to use descriptive rather than judgemental language in the feedback that they give and they will need to listen very carefully to the views of the other party in the process of coming to a conclusion.

SELF-DISCLOSURE

Rather strangely one of the behaviours that is most likely to provoke action is that of self-disclosure. It is often genuinely the case that individuals or groups cannot see or appreciate the situations and possibilities that face them, and sometimes they are frightened by them. In circumstances such as these it helps a great deal to hear of an equivalent situation, especially one that has bemused or frightened us but that was dealt with. Of course, in self-disclosing the facilitator must not appear in any way arrogant or dismissive of the issue that the group is facing. When handled well and in the appropriate circumstances this final behaviour is very powerful in generating action within the group.

SUMMARY

The facilitator role is increasingly recognized as a vital one in developing a significant group problem-solving capability within the organization. For it to work, those charged with the responsibility need to develop high levels of knowledge of group behaviour in general, and skill in using this knowledge, so that they can apply it to the particular situations they encounter, with all the individual differences in ability, motivation, discipline and tenacity that exist.

* * * * *

REVIEW

There is no doubt that organizations face many problems that need to be solved if they want to survive and succeed. Problem-solving groups have a central role in this. If groups use the structure laid down and if they pay attention to the advice on working together effectively, they achieve success and so help to assure the success of their organization.

As was said at the beginning of the book, we make many false assumptions about the innate skills that we have in both solving problems systematically and in working together effectively, so training is essential, at all levels. People are either selected or choose to become involved, and once they become used to the process they invariably get a lot of satisfaction from their involvement at a number of levels, solving problems and saving waste for their organization, understanding each other and working better together. They also develop skills that are just as applicable in their lives away from the workplace.

Problem-solving groups, whether 'real' or 'virtual' are at the core of the modern organizational world – use them; use them wisely; use them well!

INDEX

50 Brain Teasers

For Meetings, Presentations and Training Sessions

Graham Roberts-Phelps and Anne McDougall

You're making a presentation and you want it to start with a bang!
You're half-way through a meeting and need to give everyone a shot
in the arm! Or you're running a training session with your team and
they just don't seem to want to take part!

You've probably been in one or more of these situations, both on the
giving and the receiving end. But the next time it happens, with this
book at your disposal, you'll have a collection of 50 instant, flexible
and enjoyable solutions to draw on, to wake everyone up and get
them taking part.

Most of the Brain-Teasers require no more than a flip-chart
or OHP to run. And because they need only a few moments'
preparation you can plan them into your sessions in advance, or
simply introduce them to fill any gaps, help raise energy levels
or signal a change of direction.

Whatever the audience you're working with, this collection is
guaranteed to get their attention.

GOWER

Made-to-Measure Problem-Solving

Victor Newman

Do you solve problems in the style of a coyote, competitor or eagle? Recognising the way you approach and deal with problems at work will enable you to identify the most suitable technique to use on a daily basis.

Victor Newman's practical book strikes at the heart of fundamental challenges faced by all managers. It looks beyond the conventional techniques of problem-solving to the underlying process, identifies eight stages and explains how to recognise which technique is appropriate to which stage. On this basis managers can generate solutions at both the personal and the organisational level.

A unique feature of the book is a Problem Solving Styles Profile that enables each reader to apply the material in the text to improve their own problem-solving capability.

GOWER

Best Practice Creativity

Peter Cook

The ability to generate new products and services is emerging as one of the few sources of competitive advantage. There is no shortage of books on personal creativity or collections of creativity techniques. What makes Peter Cook's approach unique is its strategic perspective. He is concerned with ways of developing organizations where creativity is valued and systematically encouraged.

Drawing on both the published literature and the experience of a wide range of organizations, he:

- describes methods of promoting creativity in organizations
- summarizes established concepts and practices on the subject
- examines the role of leadership in organizational creativity
- looks at organizational structure as a source of creativity
- sets out principles for the design of problem-solving processes
- presents a critical guide to creativity techniques.

Throughout the text there are 'activities' to help readers identify and analyse potential improvements in their workplace, and the book concludes with '101 ideas for increasing organizational creativity'.

In a world where turbulence is the norm, 'business as usual' is probably the route to extinction. For any executive or functional manager determined to find 'a better way', Peter Cook's stimulating and practical book will repay careful study.

GOWER